Anonymous

A Summer Trip across the Continent

Anonymous

A Summer Trip across the Continent

ISBN/EAN: 9783337149147

Printed in Europe, USA, Canada, Australia, Japan

Cover: Foto ©Andreas Hilbeck / pixelio.de

More available books at **www.hansebooks.com**

A Summer Trip

ACROSS

The Continent !

INTRODUCTION.

OUR TRIP across the Continent was the culmination of the hopes of a number of years, and the devouring of everything obtainable which related to any part of it. Several of our friends had been over the route and their report only intensified our desires; and we now feel that they like ourselves did not tell half the truth. We had some misgivings as to our ability to bear the exhaustion of so long a journey, as we had only a few weeks before arisen from a dangerous and protracted illness. So not attaching ourselves to any party we resolved to go as far as our strength would bear, and return if we found it to fail; but we grew stronger and except the temporary indisposition of Mrs. B. we came through safely.

The material composing these pages appeared in the *New Holland Clarion* from January 17th to May 16th, inclusive, by request of the editor, stimulated by the inquiries of many friends, and besides our story was too long to be transmitted verbally or by personal letter. Some of the readers suggested the desirability of having the narrative placed in a more convenient and permanent shape by its publication in pamphlet form. That it has been so kindly received by the readers of the paper is very flattering and we hope has added to the subscription list, for our efforts were gratuitous.

The present is a reprint from the *Clarion*. The typographical errors (the most serious of which are elsewhere pointed out) must be charged to the devil's (*Clarion's* devil) account; the others we claim as our own and these latter ones are not few. The devil and we are good friends and will pool the account.

We have no apology to make for any of the material offered unless to say that we feel ourselves incapable of making some parts of it true to nature, and did we have the powers of description and the control of language to portray what we have seen, some persons not knowing us would be disposed to question our truthfulness. Different eyes see the same things very differently and to illustrate we will here mention what we were told at the dinner-station between Wawona and Medara on our return from the Yosemite Valley. At this place it is the custom of tourists on their return to register their names if they choose, and the attendants are apt to ask the travellers' impressions—whether the valley, big trees, etc., reached their expectations. We were enthusiastic, notwithstanding the intense heat (118°) rough road and clouds of dust which settled upon us with remarkable affection. The story had never been half told us; yet these people said that earlier in the season a gentleman and lady on their return were so disgusted that he wrote in the register—"Fool and Wife." They must have been hard to please; a dynamite explosion under them doubtless would not surprise them because there might be much greater ones. When *they* go again doubtless there will be a broad gauge railway and lightning express train of Pullman parlor and dining cars to the valley. That would be pleasanter, but there would not be so much fun and less romance if the stage is entirely dispensed with, though a little less of it would be very acceptable.

We have devoted considerable space to the history of the Mormons, etc.; to many this has refreshed their recollection of the incidents there narrated, and probably stated some points previously unknown to them. To the younger generation most of it is entirely new; and the recent agitation of the Mormon question has developed an interest which must make our abstract of history, creed, etc., of some present value. As to the righteousness or iniquity of these people in the past or present we do not judge; we were kindly received and treated

ON June 21st, 1884, Mrs. Beecher and myself left Philadelphia at 2:15 p. m., from the Broad street station, Pennsylvania Railroad, for the west. The day was glorious and the ride delightful, passing the magnificent suburban residences and towns until Malvern was reached, where on the right of the railroad the beautiful Chester Valley came into view; and from the elevation of the road presented a magnificent scene. The farms with which it is covered appeared in the distance like garden plats, the regularity of the rows of corn, still young, the even level of the fields of wheat and other grain, showing cultivation of a kind, such as, except in one other portion of Pennsylvania, we did not see anywhere else in our long trip.

After passing through the Gap, in the eastern portion of Lancaster county—"the granary of Pennsylvania"—we beheld the Pequea Valley, studded with its fine farm houses and barns, located on farms not excelled in the country for appearance, management and production. And while naturally prejudiced in favor of our own state and immediate vicinity of our birth, we will submit to the judgment of others whether they find anywhere such manifest superiority of Pennsylvania farming over that of any other part of the country. We do not in the least wish to depreciate the quality of land and the comparative amount of production of other sections, for we have seen the natural richness of the soil in other states and know their products to be immense; but with the management of the Pennsylvania farmer, their yield would be vastly increased, and with proportionally little more labor than is now bestowed upon them. I will allude to some of these points as they occurred to me in course of our trip.

Passing on through Lancaster we arrived at Columbia, once the terminus of the Philadelphia and Columbia railroad. There, fifty years ago, the freight for points west of Columbia, was transmitted to the Pennsylvania canal, and in section boats carried to the foot of the Alleghenies and by portage over their heights, thence to Pittsburg and beyond. Well do I remember these as also the Conestoga wagons used for the carriage of freight in the same direction. The contrast of then and to-day in the transportation of freight and passengers so wonderful in all particulars, and which impressed me, will be my excuse for this allusion.

At Columbia we get our first view of the Susquehanna with its high banks, broad surface and innumerable islands. Continuing our course along its banks for ten miles we arrived 6:30 p. m. at Bainbridge, a small town on a bluff overlooking the river, and in the western part of Lancaster county. Sojourning here for a few days we left June 23, 6:30 p. m. for Harrisburg, passing for twenty miles along the Susquehanna, still beautiful, majestic and grand. Waiting at Harrisburg until midnight we took the express train leaving Philadelphia at 9 p. m. for Cincinnati. Not able to procure a berth in a sleeper we were compelled to do the best we could in making ourselves comfortable in the usual day car. In the darkness we missed the view of the river, the crossing of the long bridge, the spurs of rock around which the river bends, the entrance of the Juniata into it, the Tuscarora mountains, the Juniata river and valley, the Lewistown Narrows and all that scenery which is so enchanting, always new, always interesting to the traveller, until near Altoona at the base of the Alleghany mountains. But all this we had often seen before, therefore, the regret was not so great. Too early for breakfast at Altoona we partook of a cup of coffee to bridge over the regular time of breakfast until reaching Pittsburg.

Taking on an extra engine we left Altoona and commenced climbing the grade until we reached the famous Horseshoe, at one time regarded as a marvel of engineering skill, but now overtopped by other more extraordinary ones of like character. From this point to the top of the mountains is a vast panorama of mountains and valleys seen to beautiful advantage under the rising sun as we ascend the grade. The long tunnel at Galitzin and Cresson passed, we begin our descent towards Pittsburg, having views on each side of the road, grand in their ruggedness and wildness; the valley of the Conemaugh river, the Pack Saddle, the Cambria Iron Works, at Johnstown, the openings of coal mines on the hillsides, keep the eye of the traveller busy. As we approach Pittsburg we pass the Edgar Thompson steel works located at Braddocks, the place where, in our early colonial history, Gen. Braddock was killed in a battle with the Indians, July 9, 1755, while he was on his march to attack the French Fort DuQuense, now Pittsburg. Washington, then a colonel, accompanied this expedition.

Arriving at Pittsburg at 7:40 a. m., June 24, we took a substantial breakfast and immediately thereafter took a train on the Pan Handle railroad, passing through a tunnel under the city, crossed the Monongahela river to South Side, and then on to Cincinnati From Pittsburg west the country was new to us, never having been through it before. The road passes among mountains and through forests We leave Pennsylvania, pass across the pan handle of West Virginia, and at Steubenville, Ohio, we cross the Ohio river on a high bridge. Steubenville, as many other places along the railroad where bituminous coal is extensively used, is more or less overshadowed by clouds of black smoke, which hang over it like a pall, the factories and adjacent coke ovens furnishing the most of it; the road being elevated gives a good view of the town. From Steubenville we successively passed through Coshocton, county seat of Coshocton county, and in the midst of a bituminous coal district; Newark, county seat of Licking county, on a branch of the Muskingum; Columbus, the capital of Ohio, on the Sciota river, and famous for its magnificent capitol building, Ohio penitentiary and other important buildings and institutions, factories, etc , as well as being a railroad centre; Xenia, in Green county, on the Little Miami river, all being places of some size and note.

Following the Little Miami river to near its mouth, then westward along the Ohio river we arrive at Cincinnati at 7:30 p. m., June 24 Having taken quarters in the St. James hotel on Fourth street, and partaken of supper, we sallied out to see a little of the place prior to early retiring. This city, more recently famous for its riots of last spring and the Ohio flood in February, is built upon two terraces from the edge of the river and backed by high bluffs, the tops of which are reached by inclined railways, and back of these the city extends for some distance. It has many fine buildings, more or less

blackened by the smut from the burning of bituminous coal. The streets are generally at right angles and average a greater width than those of our eastern cities. The business houses are large and commodious, and while of the latter the Gibson and Burnet House are the principal there are others whose accommodations contribute to every comfort, and the St. James is one of them.

To the casual visitor this city presents much the same appearance of other cities of the same class; the wholesale and retail business is about the same, its factories, numerous and varied in products, but here as in the various cities throughout the country we find depots for the particular productions of the adjacent country; as for instance the tobacco grown so largely in Kentucky and the lower parts of Ohio and Indiana is sent to this centre of trade as may be seen in the large warehouses where it is stored in large hogsheads awaiting a purchaser. "Blue-grass dew"(Bourbon) from the vale of Licking, finds a market here; peanuts are also found here in large quantities shipped from the south. Cincinnati is also famous for its pork-packing, its German population and the "German Nectar" commonly known as beer. The Esplanade on the site of what probably was a market shed in the city's earlier days, is elevated about two and a half feet above the street and in the centre is a large and very ornamental fountain of bronze, surmounted and having on its sides allegorical figures of the same material, and life size. The fountain is a gift of a philanthropic, public spirited and wealthy citizen. On the upper terrace, but some distance from the bluff, running in a general east and westerly direction is a canal; between this canal and the bluff is a large population of Germans and to visit them you go "across the Rhine," for the canal is commonly so called at this place. Then to "cross the Rhine" is what almost every visitor to this city expects to do. Here we see German life as it probably is in the "Vaterland," though there is nothing distinctive in the architecture. So across the Rhine we go and see beer saloons and music halls with beer attachments in great numbers and almost side by side, where, when the day's work is over, and on Sunday, the German father and mother saunter in, taking their children, and the beaux and belles are to be seen sitting at tables in perfect harmony and propriety enjoying the fluid which the mythic King Gambrinus taught them was good, and the wines which we hope had the genuine flavor obtained on the banks of the Rhine in their much loved fatherland. We saw these places, but not being accustomed to the customs of the country we did not enter, though it is said that "when you are in Rome you should do as the Romans do." Every visitor who has not visited the bluffs misses a very fine view. These bluffs about 200 feet high, are variously named in their different parts as Mt. Auburn, Mt. Adams, Mt. Washington, etc. They are reached by inclined railways and on the tops at various points are large buildings, characteristically named the Highland House and the Lookout House, generously glazed, filled with tables and chairs, as also surrounded by large platforms likewise provided with tables and chairs, and with accommodations for several thousand persons each. Here beer is dispensed and music enlivens those who of an evening ascend these heights and in the light of the electric lamps or moon, or both, enjoy an hour or two, and get a good breath of cool fresh air after a day's swelter in the hot city below. Fireworks, particularly on the Fourth of July, are set off on these heights and the view from the city is grand. From these heights in the daytime a grand view for many miles is open to the gazer. At his feet is the busy city which is much below him; it is however sometimes covered by a dense cloud of smoke so that only the churchspires and the roofs of very high buildings are seen sticking through. To the east and west he sees the winding of the Ohio river; to the south is Covington on the Kentucky side and the mouth of the Licking river. Back of these points of view are fine residences, and horse-car lines continue from the inclined railways. We did not visit the parks, theatres, etc., as change of plan prevented our return to the city. We saw no traces of the great flood and were surprised to see the great Ohio at this time, to be a most insignificant stream at this point, as compared with the Delaware at Philadelphia; indeed it seems as if one could almost throw a stone across it, but a sixty foot rise makes it an almost irresistible flood. The banks gently descend to the water's edge, are paved with cobblestones and the flat bottomed steamboats just throw off a gang plank, generally rigged to a crane near the bow of the boat and readily swing to one side or the other to load and unload. The smoke stacks, generally double, are very tall and jointed in the middle so as to permit their passing under the bridges crossing the Ohio. These boats go up the river to Pittsburg and down the Ohio and Mississippi to New Orleans, and by this means Cincinnati carries on an extensive commerce with a vast region of country. As a railway centre it is also extensively known.

Cincinnati is connected with Covington, Kentucky, by a magnificent suspension bridge of the same general pattern as that connecting New York and Brooklyn, but it is a dwarf compared to the latter. Over this bridge pass horse car tracks continuous from those in Cincinnati and continued for a long distance into Covington, so taking a car we crossed the bridge to reach the Kentucky Central railroad depot to take the train for Cynthiana.

Covington is a place of considerable size and importance, being nicely laid out and well built. If it did not lay within the jurisdiction of another state, doubtless ere this it would have been consolidated into the corporate limits of Cincinnati; as it is, many Cincinnati business men reside there and most of the commerce between Cincinnati and central Kentucky passes through it. As we only saw Covington from the horse cars we cannot say much of it.

Leaving Covington we followed the main trunk of the Licking river until we reached Falmouth, about thirty miles south, where we left it and generally followed the bank of the West Branch or Little Licking for thirty miles more, when we arrived at Cynthiana. The main river is of some length, but of no great size at this time; but when the Ohio leaves its banks the Licking is apt to do the same and makes a freshet at its outlet the more dangerous. Along the smaller branch it is of quite as insignificant a size as small eastern creeks, the result of protracted drouth. The country along the railroad is rolling, in some places decidedly hilly, with here and there patches of level ground. The land is fruitful; much is under cultivation, producing generous crops, but there is an air of indifference in the general management of the farms. The farms, generally quite large, are not cultivated to their fullest extent; more time is devoted to the raising of horses and cattle; the fame of the state for the former is well known, so that much land is kept for grazing purposes. The "blue grass," a natural growth, requires no replenishing, a field remaining unchanged for years; the generally mild climate allows pasturing in winter and unless the weather is extreme the stock scarcely requires any shelter. Rotation of crops in the soil is not regarded as necessary, and the use of straw and manure, as a fertilizer, is scarcely thought of.

Corn, wheat, tobacco and hemp are the major crops of the soil. Corn, after being husked, is often placed in rail cribs, the rails laid together as for building a log house. The ears are generally considerably longer than that grown in Pennsylvania; probably the climate influences this. Wheat either remains in the shock until threshed, or is stacked. I am informed that generally there is only enough wheat raised as is necessary for home consumption. Tobacco, a great staple, was once, if not now, regarded of a fine grade and probably would continue so if the attention was bestowed that experience has demonstrated to be of such great value in its production in our state.

The residences and farm buildings are generally unpretentious, even though their owners may be wealthy. The mansion house, generally of wood, is usually one story high, though it may cover considerable space. The barns are small and often only large enough to shelter the family horse, the farm implements often standing in the field from season to season. The negroes, of which there are plenty, live in one story shanties or log huts. We have some samples in our own state.

This is the famous "blue grass" region of which all Kentuckians, particularly those who live in it, are supremely proud, and to own a "blue grass farm" generally means that the owner is comfortly fixed. Now the grass is not blue, as the name would indicate; it is delightfully green, but at certain periods there is a bluish or purplish tint along the flower and seed stem; this grass does not grow high, and between the seeds which fall and the extension from the roots, it requires no artificial renewing and continues from year to year. It is regarded as most nutritious and the choicest Kentucky horses and cattle are pastured on its finest fields. A similar grass is found in this state, but not to any great extent, nor do I know of its being encouraged.

Another production of this particular region (though by no means confined to it) and for which it is famous is "blue grass dew" or Bourbon whisky. Distilleries are found at short intervals all along the railroad and river. Business, either in the manufacture or sale of this article, is at present in a condition of stagnation, the result of certain government requirements together with the influence of the depression in the commercial world. Much of the corn raised in Kentucky is converted into this good but often very bad (in its influences) article.

Cynthiana is the county seat of Harrison county. It is located on the Little Licking about sixty-seven miles from Covington. It is an unpretentious town; buildings generally of brick and not imposing; it contains a court house and that necessary associate a jail, banks, hotels and business houses, a good school, a number of distilleries, steam roller flour mill, etc., showing considerable business,

but at the time of our visit it was rather dull. The streets are broad and well piked, indeed all the roads in Kentucky are piked and kept in excellent condition making them a great comfort in all seasons of the year. The people here and in the surrounding country that we visited are exceedingly hospitable, carrying out the reputation of the people of the south on that score, and to be known as a friend of one of their friends means a profusion of attention.

There is a great deal of horse-back riding by both sexes. On certain days, particularly court days, many men are seen riding into town and hitching their horses to a rail which more or less surrounds the court house; then there is a great barter of stock, trading, etc. Hot blooded and impulsive, yet the morals or breaches of the law must be very slight among the people of this county, for the jail is so small that the prisoner's accommodations do not equal that of a police station house in one of our eastern cities, and from this we must infer that they do not need a larger one. Battle Grove Cemetery is located about half a mile east of the town on an elevation, and commands a beautiful view of the surrounding country; it is handsomely laid out, carefully kept and elegantly decorated with fine monuments and other appropriate markings of those buried there. During the late war this spot was the scene of a brisk skirmish. This was prior to its use as a cemetery.

In Cynthiana we sojourned some days. Here resides Mrs. Lydia B. Cook, an aged sister of my father, and the last survivor of a large number of brothers and sisters. A Pennsylvanian by birth, she with her husband and family, went to Kentucky just prior to the war, where he and three sons engaged in the distillery business, in which they were very successful. One son Cyrus B. Cook, now deceased, became the mayor of Cynthiana. His family still reside there. One daughter married Mr. Jacob Walford, a distiller and grain dealer in Cynthiana; another married Mr. W. H. Wilson, a famous horse raiser, and owner of Abdallah Park and driving course; another daughter Mrs. M. M Norris, a widower, is the leading milliner and dressmaker in the county, having the largest and finest store of the kind in Cynthiana, and whose son is editor and proprietor of the Cynthiana *Times*; Mr. William Cook also residing here is the only surviving son. From all these we received distinguished attention. Through their courtesy and kindness we were enabled to see the surrounding country, which would invite the attention of the most critical or prejudiced.

A short mile south of town, on the line

of the railroad, is the Abdallah Park. Here is as fine a race track as I ever saw, fully equipped with stables for the accommodation of some of the finest horses in the country, some owned by Mr. Wilson and some owned by others who had them there for training or other purposes. Mr. Wilson and family reside on the place. A feature of this park is, that Mr. Wilson has constructed a short track entirely under cover, where, no matter what the weather, he can gait his "one and two year olds" or show them to anyone contemplating purchase. The park is also used as a fair ground at appropriate seasons, when trotting is made a feature. Mr. Wilson is a thorough horse lover and and no trouble is too great when he has an appreciative companion. As a sample of the inhabitants of his stables I will mention Triumvir, Huron, Long Branch, Chestnut Wilkes, Tom Bagby, Ink, and others, all famous on the turf; but the pride of Mr. Wilson's heart, and, from what I heard, the pride of the whole state, is his beautiful show mare, Lady de Jarnett, who has captured the prize for beauty and style at all the fairs where she has been shown, and decorated with bushels of ribbons bestowed by admiring ladies.

Since our return home we have learned with regret that the stables and dwelling of Mr. Wilson had been burned, including the horses above named together with others, except Lady de Jarnett and another, which were on a car, just having arrived from the fair at Cincinnati, but too late to unload that night; otherwise they too would have been burned. The family of Mr. Wilson narrowly escaped, saving some furniture. A stable hand, probably the cause of the fire, was burned to death. I was taken by Mr. Wilson to several blue grass farms where he kept his brood mares and young stock; his annual sales of stock are large and well known among horsemen all over the country.

Leaving Cynthiana after a most delightful visit we passed on through Paris, county seat of Bourbon county, thence to Lexington, Fayette county. We had intended to stop and spend a few hours here, but finding the trains were not disposed to our advantage we were here but little longer than to take dinner. Long ago I had determined to visit the home of Henry Clay should I ever be within reasonable proximity. For him I cast my first presidential vote, and I longed to pay my respects by a visit to his home and his grave. Ashland is about a mile and a quarter south of Lexington, and we are informed is nearly as Henry Clay left it. His monument in the cemetery is readily seen from the railroad, a colossal statue upon a shaft of great height built over the tomb, which has an iron grating, behind which is seen the marble sarcophagus containing the body of Kentucky's greatest man, and one of the country's greatest statesmen. He should have been made president. Lexington is finely built and is the most important inland city of the state and is probably the most aristocratic city in it. It has a population of 16,000. From Lexington we went to Louisville, passing through Frankfort, the capitol, on the Kentucky river, and Shelbyville, county seat of Shelby county.

Louisville, the most important city in Kentucky, is located on the Ohio river, at the falls one hundred miles west from Lexington and one hundred and twenty-five miles from Cincinnati. Its manufactures are extensive and valuable, and its shipping interests very large by way of the Ohio and Mississippi rivers, and also by the railroads which center here. It is an extensive depot for tobacco, hemp, grain, etc. Population 123,000. Crossing the Ohio on a bridge we left Louisville for North Vernon, Jennings county, Indiana, there to intercept the train from Cincinnati to St. Louis, on the Ohio and Mississippi railroad. Passing westward we crossed the East and West Forks of the White River, and the Wabash at Vincennes.

Vincennes was originally one of a number of French trading posts established along the Wabash and other rivers, and at the lakes, to carry on the fur trade with the Indians. The country was subsequently, in 1763, ceded by France to England. This town is somewhat of a railroad center. In crossing Illinois we pass through no place of special importance till we arrive at East St. Louis. This last place is a railroad point for storage of cars and making up of freight trains for east and west. The country from Louisville is generally very level and constitutes part of the low prairie country of Indiana and Illinois. The soil is almost black, of great depth as compared with that in Pennsylvania, requiring no fertilizers and of great productiveness; corn, wheat, and tobacco, being produced in large quantities. Here there is a general air of indifference in the cultivation; straw stacks and corn shocks being left standing in the field until they rot or perhaps are burned to get rid of them; the barns are small and the houses often of only one story, generally frame, are set up on blocks two or three feet above the ground (there being no cellars). The country is so low that in the wet season the land is boggy. Cattle are raised in large numbers.

At East St. Louis we had our first view of the father of waters, the Mississippi, whose channel carries the drainage of the largest watershed in the world, from the heart of the Rockies in the far northwest, to the Alleghenies in the east, and stretching from north to south across the country. We are led to contemplate what a mighty and terrifying river it becomes when it overflows. From East St. Louis we cross the river on an iron bridge completed a few years ago by Capt. Eads, famous for his jetties at the mouth of the river. This bridge is a wonder of engineering skill, the building of the piers being attended with the greatest difficulty, which makes it figure prominently in engineering and medical annals. Passing from the bridge we enter a tunnel which goes under a portion of St. Louis. After landing we proceeded to the St. Cloud Hotel, and after resting we tried the sights, but the heat prevented much investigation. This was July 4th, and imagine our surprise to find a celebration of the day, at least by the small boy, which reminded us of other Fourths of July in Philadelphia, when fire crackers, salutes, military parades, patriotic speeches and fire works formed the features, but for several years past this anniversary is celebrated as if all the people had just returned from a funeral or that it was a day of fasting and prayer.

St. Louis is built upon two terraces above the flood line, but not backed by hills as is Cincinnati. The streets are principally at right angles N. E. S. and W. except at the upper and lower portions of the city, where they range with the curves of the river toward the N. W. and and S. W respectively. It is a railroad centre for roads from E. and N. E. running to the W. and S. W. The buildings are quite large and well built; factories are numerous; its wholesale business is extensive and its commerce on the Mississippi, Ohio and Missouri rivers is very great. Its principal hotel is the Planters, known for many years, and, in ante-bellum days, as a great rendezvous for the planters of the south. The population of St. Louis is 350,000. The Missouri river empties into the Mississippi a few miles above St. Louis; the waters of the Missouri being generally muddy, the waters of the two streams do not entirely commingle until after they have passed over a number of miles, the west half showing a muddy strip and the east half clear; the phenomenon is noticed at St. Louis.

We left St. Louis after a very short stay, pursuing our westward trip, passing suburban towns which are peopled by wealthy and other men doing business in the city, Kirkwood being the principal town of this kind and within easy access. Very soon we caught sight of the "Big Muddy" as the Missouri river is otherwise known, because it is almost always so, regardless of freshets or storms along its course. The banks of the river are backed by considerable elevations made up largely of limestone with almost perpendicular facings, and as the railroad passes along the river, view of the country back of them was cut off, except here and there where the road led the banks to avoid a large curve. We continued along the south bank of the river, crossing the Gasconade and the Osage where they empty into the Missouri, and passing through no places of particular importance until we reached Jefferson City, the capital of Missouri, in nearly the central part of the state, one hundred and twenty-five miles from St. Louis and the most important town in the interior. It is well built of stone and brick. One circumstance I will mention. On our approach to Jefferson City, but while yet some distance from it, a porter brought into the car, towels, combs, brushes, wash basins and water, to enable the traveller to wash and brush up before dinner at Jefferson City, where the train stopped twenty minutes. At no other time was this luxury thrust upon us.

Here we leave the Missouri, continuing in a general westerly direction and gradually rising, crossing rolling prairie of great fertility; corn (a little late), wheat and grass in great plenty and in fine condition, the quality of the land improving as we go. Settlements are rather thinly scattered here and there at considerable distances apart, and single houses at long intervals; indeed some are little more than shanties of probably one room; no barns for housing crops or shelter for cattle. The whole aspect of the country improves as we approach Kansas City and becomes quite attractive. Amish and Dunkers are located in this section in large numbers and their presence is noticed in the care they display in selection of land and its cultivation.

Sedalia, the first town of importance after leaving Jefferson City, one hundred and eighty-nine miles from St. Louis, is somewhat of a railroad point and of considerable business importance. Warnersburg, in Johnson county, and Independence in Jackson county are places of some note; the latter in particular, being ten miles from Kansas City, is a railroad point and is famous in the history of the Mormon emigration westward. After their expulsion from Illinois they settled at Independence and in several adjoining counties, where, after they had thought themselves secure from molestation, they were again compelled to leave by force, they being obnoxious to the other settlers; they then went to Utah. Arriving at Kansas City at the Union Depot, we secured accommodations at the St. James hotel.

Kansas City is located on the south bank of the Missouri river. It is a place of great importance as a railroad and business centre; it is well built of stone and brick on a series of terraces, more or less steep and close together, notwithstanding which they have street cars, and cable roads are in construction. Its stores rivel in size those of eastern cities; factories are numerous, and its slaughtering and packing establishments are among the largest in the country, while its stock yards have no superior for size. The union depot on the lower level near the river, is one of the busiest places in the world for its kind. Here people of all nations gather and are dispersed through the west and southwest, and this is continuous day and night. When first laid out this city was supposed to be within the Kansas line, but subsequent surveys showed that it was just east of it and consequently in Missouri; this apparently has not militated against its rapid progress; its streets are well paved and lighted. Not long ago it was the centre for a very rough element of people; now it is seemingly as polished and orderly as if established one hundred years ago. Some business is transacted on Sunday and places of amusement are open, but we saw little of it, though we were there during a Sunday. In all towns that are or have been on the frontier, there has been little regard in their early days to a consideration of the Sabbath, but certainly we saw nothing in our travels which could have offended any but bigots or fanatics. The people of Kansas City are very busy and up to the times in everything. Here we first saw evidence of the push and activity claimed for the western people, though it was not our fortune to see this everywhere even in some large cities. An extensive garden called St. James Park, where music is discoursed and beer dispensed, adjoins our hotel and is well patronized; a room on that side of the house is not agreeable to tired travelers. The hotel is finely furnished, convenient, comfortable and reasonable; let travellers take notice.

Leaving Kansas City we very shortly crossed the Kansas river on the other side of which and at its confluence with the Missouri is Wyandotte, Kansas. Following the west bank of the Missouri (for at Kansas City it bends northward) we arrived at Atchison. After changing cars we proceeded westward sixty-seven miles to Centralia, Nemaha county, in the northern part of Kansas, on the central branch of the Union Pacific. Awaiting our arrival was Mr. Abraham Brower, an old and valued friend. Mr. Brower is a Pennsylvanian by birth and for many years a resident of Williamsport, Pa. Advancing in years he felt the cares and restraints of a mercantile life as becoming very irksome; he longed for a relief which others than he have expressed and acted upon. The green fields, the open air, the horses and cattle seemed to call him, and feeling that though the air was as pure and the grass as green in Pennsylvania as in any other place, yet he seemed to think that here he would be too crowded and that he could purchase in Kansas from three to six acres for the price of one here. So riddling himself of his store he took his family and goods about five years ago and settled down on a prairie farm two miles north of Centralia. He has a fine two story frame house, his out-buildings are in true Pennsylvania style, his farm is well fenced, and there is every appearance of comfort, contentment and plenty. Our reception was most cordial and our entertainment far in advance of our expectations in a prairie home. The garden was profuse in its yield of most elegant and delicious berries and other vegetables, and the barnyard with its many spring chickens, all contributed their part in making us heartily welcome. We parted with great reluctance as from a very dear brother. May Mr. Brower and his family live long to enjoy their new home and continue to be prosperous and happy.

In all this prairie country there are few trees of any kind except along the water courses, and as the wind, having a fair sweep, rushes with tremendous velocity and often extremely cold, the settlers plant "wind breaks" of trees on one, two or three sides of the house a short distance from it, sometimes they surround the house. These "wind breaks" are very necessary to the comfort of persons and cattle.

After spending a few days with our friend and family we returned again to Atchison, from there to Fort Leavenworth, where we stopped and were royally entertained by Capt Windt, U. S. A., and his charming wife. This fort, established in 1847 to keep the Indians in subjection on the then frontier, is one of the finest posts in the country; the grounds are kept in magnificent order and cover many hundred acres, in which are numerous beautiful drives, parade grounds, rifle ranges and other means of military exercise. These grounds serve as a grand park to Leavenworth City, the people of which resort to this place for pleasure driving.

The officers houses are beautiful, commodious and tastefully arranged; here the officers and their families live, otherwise they take accommodations in a fine hotel within the grounds. There is another hotel of a different nature on the grounds to which are sent various individuals who have given offense or violated the laws of Uncle Sam, and he don't charge them anything for keeping them in victuals and clothes. Fort Leavenworth is one of the choice posts to be assigned to duty; and it is generally sought after by officers, but with all the comfort, even luxury of the place, these persons tire of it and long to have the monotony varied by an assignment to some less happily situated post and have a brush with the Indians, whom some regard as the legitimate prey of powder and ball. The case, however, sometimes becomes as with the man who went out to hunt the tiger, and returning rather precipitately it appeared that the tiger had been found and was coming after him.

Leaving Fort Leavenworth by coach we arrived at Leavenworth City. This city while having very wide streets and covering a large extent of surface, and probably doing a large business, is far from being elegantly built, or, so far as we saw, a busy place. It is probable that other places not far distant have monopolized considerable of the trade, situated as it is between Atchison and Kansas City. The country from Atchison to Centralia is rolling prairie; that between Atchison and Kansas City cannot be well observed from the cars, as the railroad passes along the Missouri and its banks are bluffy.

Returning to Kansas City we left on the Kansas Pacific railroad for Denver. Following the course of the Kansas river, the first place of importance passed through was Lawrence, forty miles from Kansas City. This place is very lively in good times, is well built, having factories, schools and university, in apparent peace with all the world. It has, however, been the scene of many acts of border ruffianism and the raid made by Quantrell during the late war, during which many persons were massacred. Population 11,000. At sixty-seven miles from Kansas City we pass through Topeka, the capital of Kansas, a city well laid out and fine buildings for business and residences; it is a railroad centre; two colleges we are informed, are located here. Train stopped twenty minutes for dinner. Population 23,000. At ninety miles we pass St. Mary's where there is a large Catholic seminary, which is finely located and enclosed; this place was originally a Catholic mission. At one hundred and three miles we pass Wamego, a place apparently

of some importance; we could learn little of it. At one hundred and eighteen miles we pass Manhattan, a town of 2400 inhabitants, and having some very imposing buildings. The next station, Junction City, is a railroad point, one hundred and thirty-eight miles from Kansas City. At one hundred and sixty-two miles we arrive at Abilene, county seat of Dickinson county.

The country through which we passed is of great fertility; corn, wheat, oats and grass are raised in great quantities and the towns passed through seem to be located in fine situations and surrounded by all that contributes to solid wealth and comfort; the farms are large and well managed, and the improvements generally of good quality. After leaving Kansas City the railroad follows the Kansas river until we reach Fort Rily at the mouth of the Republican, having crossed the Big Blue river at its mouth near Manhattan. At Fort Riley the Kansas river, as such, ceases, being formed by the confluence of the Republican and Smoky Hill; the latter which is very tortuous, we follow as nearly nearly as may be until we arrive at Abilene. A number of creeks which empty themselves into the Kansas were also crossed; as they were generally insignificant we did not note their names. I will also here say, that frequently what are called rivers in the west would in the east scarcely be regarded as more then fair sized creeks, though the rivers thus far named are of considerable size but not of any great depth. The scenery along the Kansas river, besides the fine farm country, is very curious, particularly from Wamego westward to St. George; high above the cars range curious mounds with lines (horizontal) of projecting rock on the top edges resembling breastworks made for protection and defense by the former occupants of the land. These formations are found at other points along the line further west and running for miles; they seem to be made up of a dingy or dirty limestone unlike that formed in the east.

Abilene is a town of wide streets, well built, and in as fine an agricultural country as one would wish to see. Here as well as in a large part of this county, is to be found a large population of Dunkers, mostly from Lancaster county, Pennsylvania. I need not say what they have done for this section; their peculiarities are too well known in the east, and they have lost none of them in their new homes. I feel satisfied that they will make Dickinson county one of the richest agricultural counties in the state. The product of this country has so often been written up that I should hesitate to do more than note that wheat produces from twenty-five to forty bushels per acre and other crops in proportion; this on land that, according to the improvements, costs from $25 to not more than $50 per acre, any the labor of cultivation reduced to a minimum, for no manuring is required; the same field is sown with the same kind of seed many successive years, and does not seem to weaken; no stones to be gathered, no rocks in the way of the plow, no stumps, etc., as in other new country in the east. But do not be misled by my strong statements into the belief that the whole state is thus productive, for as we go westward the country gradually gets poorer and poorer until nothing could be raised and indeed no one appears to try, for a desolation and desertion strikes the eye which is almost painful, and unknown in any part of Pennsylvania, not excepting its rockiest and wildest counties; but more of this as we get to it.

At the railroad station at Abilene is a very fine hotel of imposing exterior called the Henry House, built and owned by the railroad company. Here we stopped in the afternoon after a hot ride; the day was said to be the hottest of the season and the progress slow as compared with eastern travel. The next day I procured a pair of bronchos at a livery stable, the owner of which was satisfied with recommendations from one who had been a Lancaster county man and one who knew of me; perhaps the owner was also satisfied because I was a Pennsylvanian, and Pennsylvanians are generally of good repute in Kansas because many of the settlers are samples of our people. We, however, were the only ones who feared that the animals might not be returned in good time and order for they required urging and persuasion occasionally with the whip. Bronchos generally are good travellers. So with the bronchos and a buggy (you see they have some of the conveniences and luxuries of civilization) we set sail southward over the prairie; this was our first drive of any considerable extent; in such country where there is little fencing and the land not broken, road and field are alike comfortable to drive over because the land is level. 'Tis best to follow the road unless you know how to read the section stakes which mark the ranges, townships, sections, etc., otherwise one might readily get lost. Thus following the road after a ride of twelve miles we arrived at Belle Springs, and it would puzzle you to find either the Belle or the Springs; however, two or three houses and more in process of erection, and a post office, which as it lacked the palatial exterior of the one we have in Philadelphia, we did not see, constitute this village; whether more existed on paper than what we saw I cannot tell. Frequently these towns are all on paper, but the land is there all the same, even if it should happen to be covered with water like the town of Napoleon in Mark Twain's "Gilded Age." It is almost a wonder that this place is not called Belle Springs City, for it is a fact that many towns in the west little larger than this are given the grandiloquent title of city; probably the honest ex-Pennsylvanians would not permit the use of such misleading names.

At Belle Springs we found our nephew Mr. A. L. Hall, of Lancaster county, who had gone there last spring on a prospecting trip, and finding that he could make himself useful he settled down to work in house building, and in harvest helping his employer. His expression of satisfaction was such that, while an early return from the promised land was expected, with a report on its qualities as he saw them, his return is indefinitely postponed and will give him opportunity to quietly consider the matter of making a purchase and ultimate removal. His residence with Mr. Eli Hoffman and family, formerly of western Lancaster county, and near neighbors before they left Pennsylvania, tend to make him satisfied in a country where people are not many and neighbors some distance apart as compared with the east. I must here give testimony to the hospitality extended by Mr. Hoffman to us, and also to say that all these people are hospitable and accommodating in the extreme. We were solicited very earnestly to remain until Sunday (this was Saturday) but not calculating upon such pressing kindness and with the twelve miles return, we declined and turned our faces toward Abilene, where we arrived in the early evening. The day had been exceedingly hot—104 degrees in the shade. It will surprise the eastern people when they go west, particularly as visitors, to find how little account the people there make long distances; a ride or drive of one or two hundred miles is accomplished in a short time and really one hardly perceives how quickly the ground is covered when the country is generally level.

The next day (Sunday) Mr. Hall and a friend rode into Abilene to spend the day with us, but as our time was very short and there being nothing of any special interest to the casual visitor, besides finding that but one "through train" passed west that day, we concluded to leave rather than remain until the next day at the same hour, for the railways in the west, in consequence of the general stagnation

in business, have reduced the trains to
one "through train" a day each way;
and during the rest of our travels, both in
going west and returning to the Mississippi, we found this very inconvenient
state of affairs, preventing our stopping
a few hours here and there where we
might have seen something of interest,
but not enough to venture the loss of
twenty-four hours should it not prove
so.

Leaving Abilene in the afternoon we
continued through good country, passing
Solomon City, crossing Solomon river
near its junction with the Smoky Hill,
also crossing the Salina, proceeding on
through Salina, Brookville, Fort Harker,
Ellsworth, Wilson, Russell and Ellis, all
towns of more or less importance; at the
latter place we took supper. The crops as
we go west seem to consist more of wheat
and less of corn, as if the soil or climate
was not adapted to the perfection of the
latter. After passing Russel the country
gets poorer and poorer and is used more
for cattle herding, also horses and sheep,
for we see great numbers of them as we
pass along. Darkness covered the land
and we were left to think of the sights
thus far seen and early stowed ourselves
to rest and sleep until daybreak, for we
were at the time of closing our eyes three
hundred miles from Denver, and at daybreak had over one hundred and fifty
miles to ride before breakfast. The tired
traveller can generally sleep anywhere
and so we took it by putting together the
cushions of three seats (there not being
many passengers) because we were unable
to get a sleeping berth at Abilene. Sleep
gotten in this manner is generally much
broken, and we got the first glimpse of
morning, and consequently of the country, at a very early hour. On the prairie
and at these high elevations the morning
dawn appears much earlier than in the
east ; it may be several hours before sun-
rise.

With the break of day we found ourselves not far from Kit Carson, a station
on the railroad, named after the famous
scout and frontiersman. The station preceeding this, called First View, one hundred and sixty-seven miles from Denver,
is socalled because here on a clear day the
first view of the Rockies is obtained ; we
did not know of it at the time and besides it was two o'clock in the morning.
The country we had passed through,
we were informed, is rather thinly settled, and on opening our eyes in the
morning they fell upon a country that
could not be inviting ; a sandy soil, if
soil it can be called, gravelly and some
stones, with some sage brush. Now sage
brush is like the Jamestown weed ; it de-

lights in what apparently no other plant
could live on ; the ground consequently
is very poor, and a goat or mule would
starve to death if compelled to eat this
only vestige of vegetable life, even though
they have reputations which rival the
ostrich. But we come to places before we
reach Denver where absolutely nothing
will grow. We are crossing the great
American Desert.

In many places along the road where
we saw cattle grazing the country was
apparently so bare of grass that Mrs. B.
often said she would like to be alongside
of the mouths of these animals to see
what they got to eat. Here and there is
a rank grass called "bunch or buffalo
grass" which the cattle seemed to enjoy,
but at this season of the year it appeared
as if blasted by heat and withered for
want of water, of a color strikingly like
as if it had died from the roots; it is
claimed, however, that it is self cured and
very nutritious, but we are of the impression the cattle were making a virtue of a
necessity as there is nothing else to eat,
nor do I think any eastern cattle could be
induced to think it fit to enter their
stomachs; yet these western cattle generally looked well, and from here they
are shipped or driven to market at Kansas City, Omaha, Chicago or farther east.
This grass range or grazing belt extends
absolutely across the United States from
north to south, is many miles wide and
reaches far up on the foot-hills of the
Rockies. From Kit Carson the railroad
extends north-westerly to Denver, where
we arrived at 7:30 a. m., mountain time,
six hundred and thirty-nine miles from
Kansas City.

We had passed from Kansas City to
Denver over what was apparently a level
or gently rolling prairie, and the travel
should have been easy and rapid, but the
contrary was the case, for it was difficult
and slow. This will be explained when
I say that Kansas City is 763 feet above
sea level and from there the gradual
ascent to Denver reaches 5203 feet or
about one mile above sea level. This is a
long pull and requires a strong pull, but
is trifling in comparison to other ascents
of greater height in much shorter distances which are subsequently made in
the railway cars. The atmosphere becomes more and more rarified as we
ascend this grade ; the mountains were
seen at a longer distance than what we
would be enabled to do in the east. To
the south-west stands Pike's Peak among
the snow capped mountains as a land-
mark which guided many a weary strug-
gling adventurer or emigrant who had to
make the journey overland on horseback
or in "prairie schooners" to this newer

El Dorado just prior to the building of the U. P. R. R.

Arriving at Denver we proceeded to the Brunswick Hotel, where, after the necessary ablution, we partook of a substantial breakfast and then laid down to rest. The Hotel Brunswick we can recommend to all visitors to Denver, for comfortable accommodation, excellent and plenty of provision, agreeable and courteous attendance, and charges moderate considering quality. Denver is built on the desert prairie which surrounds it, giving an unobstructed view on the north, east, and south, for very many miles; but on the west are the Rockies, and while they are in full view from the city and appear to be scarcely more than an hour's walk away, they are from fifteen to twenty miles away. If you don't believe it and want to take a little exercise before breakfast, try a walk to them; only take your breakfast before you go, unless you want to postpone the breakfast until the next day. This deception as to distance which is general in these high altitudes is due to the rarified atmosphere and is not easy to appreciate at first.

How or why this spot should have been selected as the site of a city is not at this time easy to say. It may be a part of the unwritten history with which we are unfamiliar; it is, however, the offspring of those peculiar enthusiasms which pervade a certain class of mankind who love roving and adventure in wild and almost inaccessible places. This much we got from one of the early pioneer settlers, that "it was conceived in sin, brought forth in iniquity and was still a little wicked."

Thirty years ago there was no settlement at this point; only the prairie in its dreamy barrenness. About 1856 or 57 some prospectors announced to the world that gold was to be found at Pike's Peak, so from the settlers or rather the miners who flocked to this vicinity beginning a town with all the characteristics of mining towns, it is now a city of 75,000 inhabitants, as well built as any eastern city of its size, having some buildings of which any city might be proud, wide streets, well shaded and with running water in the gutters carried by conduits from the mountain streams which never cease to flow. Business of all kinds is carried on in buildings of considerable pretentious as to size and architecture. It has, however, been largely in the direction of out-fitting miners' camps, etc., and the receipt and shipment of the products of the mines. The private residences are, many of them, surrounded by lawns, filled with flowers; in some instances the houses are palatial, for there

is great wealth here. We saw the residence of Mrs Tabor No. 1, which is built on a plot of about four acres including the whole block, which is cultivated to about two-thirds of its extent, the whole enclosed by common board and post fence. Trees of various kinds are scattered over ground, giving it a rural appearance; the the house is of brick and quite extensive We made a call at the residence of Bishop Warren of the M. E. Church, but as he was absent from the city we did not see him.

The Tabor Grand Opera House is a large ornamental building of stone and is one of the most finely appointed places of amusement in the country. It was built by the millionaire Tabor, who also owns a large hotel in Denver. The Court House is probably the finest in the country, built since 1880, at a cost complete in furniture, etc., of $350,000. It is finished in hard woods and the floors are laid in marble tiles. We were kindly taken through by an officer and finally conducted to the dome, from which we had a grand view of the city, mountains and surrounding country for many miles. The permanent exposition building just outside of the city, is constructed on the same general plan as the Main Centennial Exposition building in 1876, only it is much smaller. Here annually are shown the products of the earth's surface and the mines of the state attracting large numbers of people. The railway depot is a large and commodious building of stone and admirably adapted to the purposes for which it had been built.

The city is supplied with all of the modern conveniences of water, gas, electricity, horse and steam street cars, etc., as in any of the largest eastern cities. Cherry river runs through the city and is bridged over at many points; it is generally a dry river (?) at this season of the year, but in times of great rains and overflow of mountain streams it is filled to a more or less extent. The South Platte river adjacent to the city, is, however, a permanent stream. Denver is the point of departure selected by most tourists for taking various excursions among the mountains and they are numerous. A certain railway guide says that the area of Colorado "comprises 104,500 square miles of mountains, canons, valleys, and plains," and the visitor wonders where the agriculture is carried on which is said to be so extensive and susceptible of still greater development.

So after resting somewhat and seeing in a quiet way, the particular sights of the city, we concluded to start out among the mountains, first having taken some letters of introduction to Mr. Geo. Ady, the obliging general agent of the U. P. R. R. at Denver, and from him we received such advice as was exceeding serviceable because the snow in the mountains even in July is not always sufficiently melted to allow easy visit to some points, and there are occasional snow slides and wash-outs that prevent the trains from running and such had occurred this spring; it is also a fact that some few much lauded places are not worth a great deal of effort to see, particularly if special trips are to be made to see them. Of some of these points we were judiciously advised.

While I shall attempt to make a description of what we saw in these excursions and may state some almost incredible facts, it will be but a faint shadow of the reality, for no man can by word or pen do justice to these wonders; they must be seen. I shall have occasion to refer to the parks of Colorado, of which there are three grand divisions, having smaller parks inside them. These three are the North, Middle and South Parks, each covering many thousands of acres and surrounded more or less with walls of high mountains. Within them are some mountains also, but generally of less altitude. The valleys in these basins are generally broad, covered with grass, fine streams running through them, furnishing fine fishing, hunting and grazing. The North Park extending from southern Wyoming southward into Colorado, a distance of probably 50 miles we did not visit; in it rises the North Platte river. Middle Park, separated from North Park by the Park View mountains, is less extensive, about sixty miles west of Denver. We got a view of a portion of it from an elevated point; in it rises the Grand river, which, uniting in Arizona with the Green river, forms the Colorado river. South Park is very large, occupying the whole of Park county and this is a very large county; the park is about sixty miles south-west of Denver; in it rises the South Platte river.

Our first trip out of Denver is to Leadville, one hundred and seventy-one miles away (but about two-thirds of that distance in a straight line) by the Denver and South Park division of the U. P. R. R., following the banks of the South Platte river, through Platte canon, over Kenosha summit to Buena Vista, then northward to Leadville. The road is apparently constructed with an eye to safety, the need of which can only be appreciated by seeing it; the steep grades, the narrow ledges, the frightful precipices, the overhanging rocks, the narrow canons, the short and frequent curves, require a solidity and strength of material, both in road and rolling stock, together with great care and management, without which destruction and death would be the frequent result. The first portion of the road passes southwest along the wooded banks of the South Platte and reaches apparently up to the face of the mountains, when with a sudden turn the train dashes into Platte canon, until then unseen in the approach. With minds prepared by previous reading we had looked for something grand and sublime, but the reality far overreached our expectations. At this point the North Fork of the South Platte emerges with a wild rush from between the granite portals of the canon. From the time of leaving Denver we proceed to ascend a grade; on through the canon the road continues upward to Kenosha summit, 10,000 feet above sea level, and nearly 5,000 feet above the level of Denver. The walls of the canon are sometimes very close together, and encroach upon the river, at other times widening somewhat, have more or less precipitous faces, very rugged, and presenting at every turn some new features. The fancy can trace faces like the "Old man of the Mountain" in the White Mountains of New Hampshire, and heads in various positions, as if they were the guardian spirits and were entering a protest to the advance of the intruder into these solitudes; or perhaps beneath the Cathedral Spires (so named from the projection skyward of slender pinnacles of rock resembling spires) are vaults unexplored wherein these spirits of the valley gather to commune. In the channel the waters of the river go bounding downward over the boulders, rushing against the rough side walls, boiling in the abrupt curves and lashed into a fury and milky whiteness in their efforts to extricate themselves from the mighty fastnesses.

With scarcely a mile of straight track in climbing on towards the summit we pass around curves so short that they are denominated "mule shoes" in contrast with the horse shoe curve in our own state before alluded to; the road-bed often on a ledge of rock no wider than just sufficient to hold it; precipices that make the hair almost stand when viewing and contemplating the result of what might happen; bridges are crossed from one side of the canon to the other, fetching up apparently against a wall, but the train dashes suddenly aside, so that for quite a while no little alarm is felt at this constant swaying of the train from side to side as it quickly and with energy passes the curves producing also in sensitive persons a sensation somewhat akin to sea-sickness. When riding along in the bottom of the canon, little is to be seen but water, the almost perpendicular walls towering up hundreds of feet, and the sky; where the walls are not too close together then the snow-capped peaks are in view when not mantled with clouds; when high up and you look down into the canon you wonder that light ever penetrates to its depths. Besides the Cathedral Spires, Dome Rock is in full view from the train; it stands out a bare barren rock from the cliff, and as its name indicates, resembles a church dome, though on a grander scale than any constructed by man. It inspires the beholder with wonder at what must be the foundation of such a mass of solid rock. At various points along the line are stations with a few cabins, much lauded as health resorts, but it is only the hunter or fisher, or some one who wants to rough it, who takes any comfort in them.

We at last reach Kenosha or Kenosha Summit 10,000 feet above sea level and seventy-six miles from Denver, rising in the last seven miles just 1,000 feet, and yet this magnificent specimen of engineering skill has greater rivals. From this height the scope of view is immense and the scenery varied and grand. With peaks above us covered with snow, we look off into South Park with its varied undulations and see fields of standing grain, vast tracks of the greenest and freshest grass and herds of countless thousands of cattle and sheep. From Kenosha Summit we descend into South Park and pass through it for forty-six miles, crossing gulches and creeks which are the sources of the South Platte river, and at a short distance beyond we reach Buena Vista, 7,957 feet above sea level and 2,000 feet below Kenosha; here we take the Denver and Rio Grand railroad and proceed northward to Leadville following the Arkansas river which takes its rise in the hills above Leadville. From Buena Vista to Leadville we climb the mountain sides 2,250 feet with views almost as varied as in the Platte Canon and through South Park; we pass in close proximity to Twin Lakes 8,500 above sea level and begirt by mountains, but we did not feel interested in merely seeing two bodies of water at this altitude, there being other matters more attractive. In this part of the road we see the curious and almost paradoxical condition of mountains on one side of a valley exposed to the north almost bare of vegetation and capped with snow, while on the other side of the valley the mountain sides are covered with flowers of many kinds and various colors, as numerous as field daisies and dandelions in their height in the east. Dandelion grows in this chilly atmosphere.

We arrived at Leadville in the evening, cold and tired, took a carriage to the Clarendon hotel and after supper retired early. Leadville is built upon a gentle slope at the foot of the mountain and is nicely and easily drained; immediately back of the city are the mountains, the sides covered with pine forest and tops covered with snow which is almost perpetual. The valley here is quite wide, from fifteen to twenty miles to the mountains in the west, though they appear to be within easy walking distance; to the north are high mountains, making this a sort of basin with the outlet to the south. Leadville is the county seat of Lake county and is purely a mining town, the result of the finding of the precious metals which run through all this country. It is only about ten years old, and is a wonder for location, size and population in this short period; while still rough it has become much polished within a recent period, making it tolerable for refined people; general good order prevails. Some of the buildings are substantial and of good size; many are only one story wooden buildings with wooden sidewalks. The streets in many places still have the stumps of the trees which were cut away at the time of the first settlement. The business is generally that of shipping ore, preparing and shipping bullion, the products of the mines, merchandize and miners' supplies; all the provisions consumed in this place are brought here, and it astonished us to see the young mountains of tin cans that contained meats and vegetables, which after having been emptied were thrown out on heaps. The region in this vicinity is honey-combed with tunnels and shafts in search of gold, silver and lead; these three and particularly the two last are found together. Lead, however, is the principal metal, as might be inferred by the application of the name to the town. Gulch and placer mining is also carried on in the gulches where water is plenty; the water washes the precious stuff from the mountain side, and it accumulates in the bottom, where it is gathered up. Earth supposed to contain gold is carried to these streams and washed in pans and the gravel, etc., is then examined to see how it "pans out." Where there is apparently considerable mineral the stream is interrupted by a series of low dams which permit of the accumulation of the gravel while the finer particles are washed farther down the channel. From these dams extend flumes, which are wooden troughs about two and a half feet wide and twelve to eighteen inches deep; in these are transverse narrow strips of wood over which the water runs. These flumes often extend many miles. Men in rubber boots and pants stand in the dams, and with picks and shovels keep stirring the water, throwing out the larger rocks as they come across them and piling them up on the bank. The fine particles of gold and silver are floated into the flumes and there the stream is broken by the strips of wood in them; in the depressions made by them mercury is placed, which, having a great affinity for gold and silver, takes up the particles. At the end of the season they have what they call a "wash up," the quicksilver is collected, the separation is made and then only is it known whether the season has been one of profit or loss. Streams are sometimes turned from their beds and the bottom worked over. Hydraulic mining is not carried on to much extent in Colorado. This is done by playing a stream of water under great pressure against a hillside containing the metal and thus washing it loose. It is in reality but a form of placer mining, but with more extended application. We went to the mouths of several mines, but did not enter them. A road, one of the roughest I ever saw, with dust twelve to eighteen inches deep, is the only one to the mines, and it is over this road that the ore is brought into the city. We did not enter because they were bringing out ore from one, the shaft of which was down a steep inclined plane and we would have been in the way; at another a perpendicular shaft of several hundred feet offered no inducement to try, and a third, probably the richest of these, had just inside a closed door, over which were a skull and cross bones, very suggestive of "no admittance except at your own peril." In another mining district, however, we did enter a mine, and of that I will speak later on. The out-put of ore at Leadville is at present quite small on account of the low price of lead in the east which makes it unprofitable to mine, but pay mineral is almost inexhaustible in this region, making Leadville permanent.

The Harrison smelter on the edge of the city is an immense affair. Here much of the ore is carried and reduced to metal, which is transported to Denver, Omaha or St. Louis for separation. The smelter is built on the same principle as an iron furnace, only the stack is not so large, generally there are several. The ore, of which we saw great piles at the smelter, bears no resemblance to the metals which it contains and the richest is often that which is apparently of the least value for any purpose whatever, and by the uninitiated would be regarded as rubbish.

We did not visit the Mountain of the Holy Cross, north-west from Leadville, requiring about twenty-five miles of rail-

roading and eighteen miles staging, if passes on the mountains were clear of snow, and of that we were not assured; besides it was not known whether the mountain was sufficiently clear of snow to see the Cross at this time. The mountain itself is not ascended, there being no trails, and it is 14,176 feet above sea. It is viewed from an opposite range several miles off, and can be seen from certain elevated points nearly one hundred miles away. It is called the Mountain of the Holy Cross in consequence of two immense fissures near the top and running transversely to each other, making a cross. The longitudinal one is said to be 1500 feet long, 50 feet wide and 50 to 100 feet deep; transverse fissure is about 700 feet long; the winter snows fill these fissures and cover the mountain top, but when the summer's sun melts the snow on the mountain, then the snow remaining in the fissures shows the white cross; this is never entirely melted out. If the summer should happen to be late the Cross is not seen until late, and that we feared was the case this season. Had the early Spanish missionaries seen this mountain, they doubtless would have established a monastery here. At Leadville we noticed the influence of the high altitude upon ourselves in a tendency to fullness of the head, headache, flushed face and hurried respiration. This would probably have not been so marked had we been entirely quiet and been here some time before starting out, but we had come to see the place (not to stay) and did some hill climbing on foot, which, under more favorable circumstances would have been sufficiently trying.

From Leadville we retraced our steps to Buena Vista and spent the night. At this place is a fine hotel and some other buildings of fair proportions, but is mostly made up of one story shanties, as in all the very young western towns, particularly in the mining region. At 5 a. m. we left for Gunnison, seventy miles west by south, and at 7:40 a. m. we stopped at Alpine for breakfast. Alpine consists of a small railroad station and a log house, indeed it seemed no place for a traveller to dine, but we were prepared for this apparently forbidding condition while we were in Denver. We ventured into the log house, found everything clean and tidy, and a breakfast awaiting, the recollection of which even now makes my mouth water, and as you may suppose a two and a half hours ride among these mountains and this delightful bracing atmosphere, made appetites prepared for anything; but here is the bill of fare—mountain trout broiled to a turn, lamb chops sweet and tender, hot cakes and biscuits, delicious coffee and cream, with fresh raspberries to finish ; and to consume all this we were allowed quite thirty minutes. On all the roads west from Denver there is liberal time allowed for meals, which is a great comfort, particularly if the coffee, cakes, etc., are served very hot, as they seem intentionally to be at many places in the east, with only a few minutes allowed to consume them.

The train continues in its upward journey among the Rockies, and at Hancock 10,939 feet is reached ; then on to the Alpine tunnel 1773 feet long, at an elevation of 11,623 feet. In the thirty-two miles from Buena Vista to the tunnel we make a rise of 4,032 feet, and have Chalk Creek below us with all the peculiar and varied scenery of this region. Alpine tunnel is on the divide in the Saguache Range and it is poetically stated that two drops of water hanging together in an uncertain manner to the roof, drop to the floor and according to the fact of their falling at one place or another, one goes eastward to the Gulf of Mexico and the other westward to the Gulf of California, and thus by circumstances pre-existent their courses are widely divergent, probably never to come together again. What a lesson in the everyday life of humanity! There are over six hundred feet of rock above the tunnel. The building of the tunnel was accomplished with great difficulty and cost, and was made to open the Gunnison country, which is rich in valuable mineral.

From Hancock to the tunnel we are above timber line, surrounded by barren rocks, and snow two to eight feet deep along the tracks and ten to twelve feet deep at the tunnel. At the western end of the tunnel we enter a snow shed where the train stopped twenty minutes for water. We took the opportunity to do a little snow-balling and face-washing, the other passengers participating ; here the snow is perpetual. Snow-sheds are necessary at some points along the line, for from the steep mountain sides plunge masses of snow, carrying huge boulders with them, irresistible in their force and carrying all before them. These sheds are sometimes very effective in diverting these masses over the cliff, but notwithstanding the sheds are built of thick round timber bolted together and fastened to the rock by two inch iron rods, the whole structure is sometimes carried away breaking rods and beams as if only made of candy. We saw workmen recovering portions of wrecked snow sheds which laid several hundred feet below the bed of the road. Numbers of snow sheds cover the railroad where it passes along the mountain side in the Chalk Creek

Valley and make the traveller think he is in a tunnel.

Beginning our descent, at three miles from the tunnel we reach Woodstock, where, a year or two ago, the whole town was swept away by a snow slide or avalanche, and some fifteen lives lost : we saw what was left of this unfortunate place. By zig-zagging along the irregular mountain sides we gradually descend into Quartz Creek Valley, along which we saw such cities (?) as are all along the line, the houses of which are frequently if not generally of rough logs piled to a little above the height of a man, with logs placed across the top for a roof, and these are covered with brush and turf. In the turf, when moist, numerous flowers are seen growing. We have seen many such buildings covered with most beautiful flowers. Whitewash and paint are almost unknown in Colorado except on the more important buildings. This gives the towns (even though of some size) a decidedly dull appearance. At Quartz, a station 10 miles from Alpine Tunnel, through the kindness of the conductor I got on the engine and had a ride of sixteen miles. The opportunity thus given, afforded one of the finest views of the trip, which can only be given to all passengers by the introduction of open observation cars. The conductors are most affable and readily give information to travellers whether solicited or not.

At 11:50 a. m. we arrived at Gunnison, 7,582 feet above sea level and seventy miles from Buena Vista. Gunnison, county seat of Gunnison county, is located in a narrow basin entirely barren, surrounded by high mountains. A more uninviting spot for a town would be hard to select, and why it was located here is almost as hard to tell. People in the east are led from various sources, to believe that Gunnison is one of the wonders of Colorado for size (considering age), activity, business interests, etc., but a more dead place does not exist within the boundary of the state. The "son of a gun" who located it is probably dead and I believe Lieut. Gunnison, after whom the town, the adjacent river and the country beyond were named, is dead too. It is well laid out, the buildings are not numerous and are most unpretentious except the hotel, The La Veta, a large and magnificent new brick building, the accommodations of which are very superior and the rates remarkably low, though transient rates are advertised at three to four dollars per day. Business in general is almost at a dead stand still and few persons are to be seen on the streets. Perhaps the people were hunting or fishing, for the hotel cards say this is "an excellent moun-

tain resort for hunting and fishing." I
should think it an excellent place for
hunting, but you want "seven league
boots" to get over the mountains, otherwise you are apt to "get left." Fossil
Ridge and West Elk Mountains are in
sight and it might be that unless you
were well provided, that "you would
have to sleep on a boulder and pull the
clouds down over you" as somebody has
suggested.

On our way to this place we passed
peaks having various names, but we did
not note them. In addition to the points
of interest already mentioned I neglected
to speak of our passage over the famous
Alpine Pass near the tunnel. The railroad is built on a narrow ledge of
rock against the mountain, only wide
enough for one track, narrow gauge at
that, with perpendicular walls of solid
granite, hundreds of feet above, and on
the other side you can look down many
hundreds of feet below, while the view
off in the valley is awfully sublime. The
Palisades on the western decline present
views which are second only to those of
the Alpine Pass, and the Hair Pin curve
of the railroad on the same side strikes
the observer with astonishment. You
are in a narrow deep gulch, where, as the
road courses along one side you look out
and see the road just below on the other
side, which is reached by making a curve
so short that it is called a "hair pin."
Except as to the degree of the curves we
were frequently, almost constantly going
over such windings both in the ascent
and descent. We were awe-inspired at
what we saw, and now after the excitement is over and calmly contemplating
all the scenes and incidents we are lost in
wonderment at the marvels of nature and
the astonishing results of man's ingenuity,
skill, perseverance and labor in the face
of almost insurmountable obstacles. This
country just passed through as might be
supposed from the description given, produces nothing for the sustenance of man.
Everything must be carried into it; a little pasture here and there for a few horses
may be found. Silver, gold and lead are
about the only productions. But our
story is far from finished; we have more
to see and more to say.

We left Gunnison, having done it very
thoroughly and in a very short period of
time, very soon reaching the gulches of
the Tomchi river, a branch of the Gunnison river, surrounded by snow clad rocks.
One side of the valley was entirely barren while the other was green with pine
trees, small shrubs and innumerable
flowers of many varieties in full bloom.
At Sargeant thirty-nine miles from Gunnison, we stopped for dinner. Here we

took on a large engine and commenced a
steep ascent until seventeen miles farther
on Marshall pass is reached at an elevation of 10,850 feet having passed through
one snow shed after another for many
miles, going along precipitous mountain
sides with frightful precipices and overhanging rocks. This is ground and lofty
climbing, but a tumble over one of these
precipices would make "lofty and ground
tumbling." Our stop is made in a snow
shed nearly a mile long, with snow and
ice on all sides. We are also on another
divide, which is very marked. I got out
of the train and placed one foot on the
descent toward the Atlantic and the other
foot on the descent toward the Pacific.
At 4:30 p. m. we leave Marshall Pass and
the next twenty-five miles is one of wonder, almost horror. The scenes we have
passed over seem to be here reproduced
in an exaggerated form if that were possible; bridges spring from one mountain
side to another, crossing almost unfath-
omable chasms, descending to Salida,
which lays in a basin of the Rockies in
the valley of the Arkansas.

Salida is the junction point of three
railroads and is quite a smart place. The
hotel at the station is called Monte Cristo.
It is owned by the railroad company and
is very comfortable. Here we spent Sunday quietly resting. The town itself pos-
sesses nothing particularly interesting.
July 21st, Monday, we left, descending
along the Arkansas, through the valley
of which, in some places, is sufficient
bottom land to allow of some cultivation
of wheat, oats and grass by means of irrigation. We pass a number of small
stations, many coal pits and few habitations, mostly cabins. The mountains
on both sides are tall and gray, and as we
approach the Grand Canon the mountain
peaks with very craggy sides increase till
they reach thousands of feet above the
track which winds in and out along their
sides with not five hundred yards of
straight track for twenty miles, the rocks
often overhanging the track and train,
with the river just at the edge.

At Park Dale, a small station forty-six
miles from Salida, we enter the Royal
Gorge of the Grand Canon of the Arkansas. I cannot do it justice; words fail at
the hands of anyone. A cleft in the
mountain, in many places thirty or forty
feet across at the bottom, with perpendicular and overhanging walls 2000 to 3000
feet high, that the gloom of evening per-
vades at midday, for the sun scarcely
penetrates to the bottom of this awful
crevice. We travel three or four miles as
it were through a dimly lighted tunnel,
for on looking up the walls seem to almost
come together and only a very narrow

streak of light can be seen. The feeling
is one almost amounting to awful dread.
The road rests on a ledge of these perpendicular walls, the rock having been blasted
away for that purpose. At one point an
iron bridge extends across the gorge from
wall to wall and braced like the rafters in
a comb roof, and from these rafters the
bridge hangs. This bridge as also a portion of the road was built by workmen
being left down from the top, and, swing-
ing in chairs, attacked the rocky sides
and gained a foothold. The river is full
of the rock blasted off to make the road-
bed and which could not then be removed.

Up, up, up, is rock, rock, rock, for
nearly 3000 feet, while down below is the
Arkansas, roaring and surging in this
narrow pass. Almost deafened with the
noise of cars and roaring waters we felt
our littleness in the presence of the wonders of God and the ingenuity and skill
of man. Going ten miles through this
gorge we leave it at Canon City and come
upon the open valley, the road following
the river to So. Pueblo and from there
northward to Manitou. The country
from Canon City to Manitou is mostly
barren except where irrigation is carried
on. Canon City has long been known as
a health resort on account of springs,
climate and air; there are also works of
various kinds, and a depot for the shipment of coal which is mined in the
vicinity and which is of excellent quality.
Colorado has extensive coal deposits
which are relatively as valuable as they
are necessary in all the extensive mining
and other operations of the state.

From Salida to South Pueblo is ninety-
seven miles, from South Pueblo to Manitou
is fifty miles. From Canon City to South
Pueblo we pass numerous castellated
rocks on the mountain range, often continuing for miles together, with here and
there a break, resembling massive
masonry, the stones being in parallel and
even tiers as if they composed the walls
of an extensive fortification. South
Pueblo is a place of considerable size and
importance, being a railroad point, with
car and repair shops, etc.; we did not
stop here. From South Pueblo we go
northward to Colorado Springs, following
the banks of the Fountain creek, a branch
of the Arkansas, which it joins at South
Pueblo. The road passes through a sandy
desert; on the west, varying from five to
ten miles distant, the front range of the
Rockies is in view, with Pike's Peak over-
topping all. Numerous buttes are also
seen on the plain; these are elevations
of various sizes and shapes, generally of
rock and making no pretentions to being
mountains. They are seen very fre-

quently all along the various roads in the
west and often present very curious ap-
pearances. In the distance they resemble
the remains of forts, or of towers, like the
ruins of some of the feudal castles on the
Rhine in Germany. One incident of this
part of our trip was a sand storm, which
came up very much like what we
sometimes see in the east in the wind
and dust just preceeding the rush of a
violent summer thunder and rain storm,
only without the thunder and rain; the
sky for a short time became hazy, then
the wind sprang up, and a noise resembling mild hail came from the car roof.
The conductor and brakemen rushed in
closed all the windows; then followed a
shower of sand in the furious wind, the
dust entering all the crevices; this lasted
only a few minutes. I have no doubt
that the overland travellers through these
western deserts have had experiences
such as we see pictured in our geog-
raphies and books of travel as occurring
to the caravans on the Arabian and
African deserts.

We also saw along this road communi-
ties of prairie dogs, wonderful, comical
and interesting. Out on the plain where
nothing grows that we could think would
serve the purposes of these little creatures
they exist by thousands. They are seen
scampering about and in a most impudent
way sit upright and motionless upon their
haunches, staring at the passer, but
should a motion be made at all aggressive
or intrusive, then quick as a flash they
drop into their holes and are gone. They
are also difficult to shoot on account of
their rapid movements. Around each of
their holes for a radius of three feet there
are planted apparently by them a stockade of sunflowers from eighteen to thirty-
six inches high, and within this stockade
the utmost apparent cleanliness and good
order prevails. At other places along the
U. P. R. R. we saw great numbers of
these interesting little creatures. I will
here say that we saw at various times,
acres upon acres of sun-flowers growing
wild like field daisies between Kansas
City and Denver, and from being quite
large at the former place, they gradually
decrease in size of plant and flower until
in Colorado the flowers would not average
three inches across.

At Colorado Springs we took the train
in waiting for Manitou, five miles westward. We were soon meandering between the foothills of the front range, and
after passing close to the Garden of the
Gods, arrived at our destination, nestled
in among the mountains, at 5:30 p. m.,
and stopped at the Barker House, a fine
cottage hotel, exceedingly comfortable
and well managed. After shaking off

the sand of the desert and a good wash, we took tea and had an hour's walk before retiring. Manitou is located on Fountain creek, a clear and swift running stream which supplies the town with water and has its rise in the adjacent mountains. It is a small, quiet town of about five hundred inhabitants; it has several fine hotels of considerable size, churches, schools and private residences; most of the buildings are of wood built on the cottage plan, very neat and apparently comfortable. The business portion of the town is rather inconsiderable. Trees are planted along the sidewalks and flowers adorn the yards of the residences. Manitou is a very busy place during the summer months, because it is a summer resort for the people of Denver, invalids and tourists. The springs, iron and soda, which are numerous, furnish an attraction. There are convenient bath houses connected with these springs; one in particular is a large two story building, very ornamental, fitted up in almost extravagant style in dressing rooms, parlors, etc. This place should have been called Colorado Springs and Colorado Springs should have been called Manitou or something else because there are no springs there.

While the middle of the day may be very hot, as soon as the sun gets past meridian the temperature is more comcomfortable, and at night a blanket or two to sleep under will be required. This last is a luxury as compared with some of our eastern experiences in mid-summer. There is a great deal of camping out on the mountain slopes, and from the town tents may be seen in every direction. They are occupied by invalids and others who are after the pure and undefiled mountain air. These tents are sometimes used far into cold weather.

Immediately out from Manitou, among the mountains, are short canons, the most noted of which are Williams and Cheyenne, Manitou Trail, Ute Pass, Garden of the Gods and Glen Eyrie, which, together with mountains, small parks, springs, etc., furnish varied amusement to carriage parties or those on foot. After breakfast the next day we engaged a two horse carriage with driver and guide and visited the Garden of the Gods, Glen Eyrie, Williams' Canon and Ute Pass. The Garden of the Gods doubtless derives its name from some Indian legends of the spirits or manitous. It is a generally level basin surrounded by high walls of rock, showing all manners of colored strata, and in nearly all positions, justifying the belief that there had at one time been an upheaval by a very great force. The surface of the basin has profusely scattered over it rocks made up of parallel and hor-

izontal layers of different densities of a reddish sandstone which have taken all sorts of shapes by the action of running water, resembling pillars with capitals, huge mushrooms, even fantastic shapes, and are named according to certain resemblances, as Wild Irishman, Punch and Judy, Mother Grundy, etc. They vary in size from a few feet to several hundreds, one reaching three hundred and thirty feet. The larger ones are known by different names and are generally denominated as "Gods." Perhaps they were regarded as visible evidences of their spirits or manitous by the Indians. The gateway of this garden is an opening in the rock probably one hundred feet wide, the rock on each side being stratified, of various colors, as red, yellow, white, etc, standing on edge and nearly four hundred feet high, the jagged upper edge resembling a saw with irregular teeth. Just inside the portal and midway between the two walls is a lone rock of considerable size, but small as compared with the height of the gateway. It seems as if placed to direct the visitors to the right or left at ingress and egress. While passing through the garden we saw in the face of one of the walls what appeared to be the impress of the complete skeleton and antlers of a large buck deer and it is called the Buck. On one of the sides of the portal is a form of the rock resembling a lion with his foot on a seal, and is called the Lion and Seal. A similar formation resembling the upper parts of a woman in a sitting posture is the Lady of the Park. Balance Rock or Pivot Rock is an irregular ovoidal mass stratified in hard and soft layers and of a reddish color. It is twenty-five feet or more in height, stands on its smaller end and appears as if it might be easily upset. It is gradually crumbling away and will eventually tumble over, but not in many years. A little grass is seen here and there through the Garden and some grass and a few scrub trees are seen in the crevices of the rocky walls.

This strange, wierd place is difficult to describe. It is visited on moonlight nights by romatic individuals, and I have no doubt the imagination could be brought to see more strange and fantastic forms in the shadows than are apparent in daylight. Monument Park, very near here, is one of the same character; we did not visit it. Glen Eyrie, adjacent to the Garden of the Gods, is a valley between the mountains, full of beautiful scenery and curious rock forms. One of the latter, a column called Major Domo is twenty-five feet high and two and a half feet through; it stands alone and resembles some of the stone monuments attributed to the Druids in Europe. In Glen Eyrie is the beautiful country residence of General Palmer, formerly the president of the Denver and Rio Grande railroad. From here we drove to Williams' Canon, one of those numerous clefts in the mountains, about three miles in length, with towering side walls of rock widening out as they go upward, but in some places at the bottom so narrow that the hubs of the wheels almost touch the rock on each side. The road which is very poor is so narrow and in such precipitous places that it is impossible for two vehicles to pass except at points where there are turnouts. A very small stream runs through the canon. The scenery is very grand but not of that sublimity of the Platte and Grand Canons. Our attention was called to an eagle's nest high up on an inaccessible shelf of the rock wall of this canon. I mention this only because eagle's nests are not often seen even by hunters. On one side of the canon, far up and reached by a long flight of steps, is the opening of the Cave of the Winds, said to be magnificent with stalactites and stalagmites; but having visited Luray Cave two years ago, we did not think this could exceed that in splendor, so we did not go in. We had come to visit such of nature's wonders as the east did not possess. From Williams' Canon we went to Ute Pass. This was an old Indian trail to points farther in the mountains and during the Pike's Peak and Leadville excitement it was the road over which the camp trains reached those places. Going as far as the Grand Falls we took a drink of pure mountain water, and doing the same at an adjacent Iron Spring we returned to Manitou.

Manitou Park, reached by the Ute Pass is a pleasant summer resort and has a fine hotel, but we did not visit it. The Seven Falls in Cheyenne Canon we did not visit; they are said to be very interesting and picturesque, but not large and grand. Pike's Peak thirteen miles away, ever in sight, is one of the great attractions of this vicinity. Manitou Trail leads to it, but as it is only reached by horse-backing, the rest on foot and a portion of the trail dangerous, though visitors generally after their return from the peak do not give expression to the fear they experienced on the narrow road, and the awful precipices they pass, where a single misstep of mule or horse means death, we did not venture, though at first intending to do so. Parties starting out in the morning from Manitou return in the evening, making a round trip of twenty-six miles. A railroad to the peak is in contemplation or in process of construction, which when complete will out-rival that on Mt. Washington or the Rigi in Switzerland. A government meteorological station is on top and sometimes in winter communication with the town is cut off for several weeks, by the snow storms; such was the case last winter, when two of the three persons who remain there came to town for provisions, etc., leaving one behind, a snow storm prevented their return for two weeks; the trails were covered and hidden; the telegraph wires were broken, but after several efforts they reached the top, gladly finding their companion alive, while they had feared he would be starved or frozen to death.

From Manitou we went to Colorado Springs leaving the mountains behind us. No springs are here except those from pipes or irrigating canals, which carry the town's water supply. It is a finely built place, the houses being generally of wood. There are several fine hotels, the largest and best of which is The Antlers, built of stone and one of the finest in the state. The streets are wide, well shaded with cotton-wood trees and water coursing along the curbs. This water is also used for irrigation of gardens, etc., containing beautiful flowers. The water supply for domestic and other purposes comes from Fountain Creek, which is carried by ditches along the mountain sides from Manitou over thirteen miles. Where irrigation is not used the prairie is barren. Little rain falls here and that generally in July and August. The average of snow and rain for the year amounts to fifteen inches.

Colorado Springs is a beautiful place and a resort in summer for persons living in adjacent places, tourists and invalids. The clear, rarified atmosphere of this vicinity is regarded as very salutary in pulmonary diseases, and is considered with more favor even in winter than the warm moist atmosphere and low ground of Florida or other southern states. The condition of society is about all that can be desired, schools, churchs, etc., are numerous and the communication with the rest of the world frequent and easy. Our stay in Colorado Springs was of short duration and taking a train on the Denver and Rio Grande railroad, we left for Denver, seventy-five miles north, passing along a branch of the Fountain Creek and a branch of the South Platte river, along which we saw horses, cattle and sheep by thousands.

July 24, we left Denver by the Colorado Central railroad for Black Hawk, Central City, Georgetown and Gray's Peak. We crossed a prairie country for about twenty miles, generously cultivated by irrigation, producing fine wheat, oats and corn. A short distance from Denver we pass the Argo smelter, one of the largest in this state. The first place of any importance on this line is Golden, at the mouth of Clear Creek or Tough-cuss Canon. It is a very busy place, built of brick and frame and surrounded by buttes several hundred feet high, upon which it to some extent encroaches. Here are smelters and iron works of fair proportions. I must here relate a little incident, somewhat serio comic, connected with this place as having occurred to Isabella L. Bird, an English lady, who in 1873 went through the canons and over the mountains of Colorado principally on horseback. "Passing by a bare and desolate looking cemetery, I asked a sad-looking woman who was leaning on the gate if she could direct me to Golden City. In doleful tones she said 'Oh, go to the minister; I might tell you, may be, but it's too great a responsibility; go to the ministers, they can tell you!'" I might remark in passing, that cemeteries are not plentiful in Colorado, that is so far as we observed. Occasionally we saw small private burial places on some of the farms, just as we find them occasionally in the east. It is stated that the famous P. T. Barnum (Greatest Show on Earth) in a lecture on Colorado, said : Why, Coloradoans are the most disappointed people I ever saw. Two thirds of them come here to die, and *they can't do it.* This wonderful air brings them back from the verge of the tomb, and they are naturally exceedingly disappointed."

But to return to our journey ; we continue along Clear Creek, enter the canon, and at Fork Creek we turn to the right in a gorge and follow it to Black Hawk, the first mining town of any importance, 8057 feet above sea level and nearly 3000 feet above Denver. Black Hawk lies in a narrow ravine in the mountains, which surround it on all sides, and with numerous mines scattered over their surface. The ore is carried to the town and if not reduced there, it is shipped by rail to other places for that purpose. It is a busy place when mining is in full operation. The houses have no level ground to be built upon and their gables are facing the few streets there are, presenting a curious appearance. This latter is the case in most of the mining towns. Five hundred feet higher up on the mountain, but almost joining Black Hawk, is Central City. By straight line they are about one mile apart, by wagon road two and one half miles, but by railroad the distance is four. Now, laying railroads in the Rockies is no joke, for the cost and engineering skill is simply enormous where the grades are so steep. The railroad connecting these two places is called the Zig-Zag, and it is just what its name indicates. Starting out from Black Hawk for a short distance the train backs up a steep grade to a certain point, when by turning a switch it goes forward and upward to another point; it then backs up another grade to a third point, then forward and upward to Central City. This is zig-zagging back and forth on the hillsides and not ascending by curves. It is, in fact, a switch back road. It fills one with astonishment; how little one man is in this great world, but what power he displays in the intelligence his God has given him.

We arrived at Central City, forty miles from Denver, in the evening, having passed numerous mines, some in apparently almost inaccessible places, both up and down the hill side. The openings in the distance look like the opening of burrows made by animals and the men could only be distinguished as such by powerful glasses. We also passed various stampers and washers. These are composed first of hoppers made of iron, into which the ore is placed, and stamps weighing many hundred pounds each, arranged in rows, are raised and let fall by machinery, thus crushing the ore into fine particles After the crushing the ore is placed in large kettles of iron having agitators, in the bottom of which is metallic mercury ; then water is run into these kettles and by agitation the gold and silver are combined with the mercury from which they are subsequently separated, and the rock and dust washed away. Even this waste water, when it reaches the gulches is again worked over, and we saw at various points, Chinese and others up to their waists in water, stirring it up, and carried on as in the description of placer mining before mentioned. The mines in this district are of great richness and extent, though little was doing at the time of our visit.

The next day after breakfast we started out on a mountain climb of about one mile to visit the Bonanza Tunnel, where we met by appointment Mr. Beck, who is part owner and manager. This tunnel extends over 1300 feet in a straight line with drifts or entries on both sides penetrating from 300 to 600 feet each. As its name indicates it is indeed a bonanza Millions have been removed from it and the supply seems inexhaustible. Procuring lanterns we entered with Mr. Beck, and saw sights which rivalled the beauties of the grottos and caverns of the Arabian Nights, the quartz crystals sparkling as gems with the precious metals in various combinations as sulphurets, etc., studded the mass. We went to the face of the mine at the end of the tunnel and there saw and touched our shadows made by the light which entered at the mouth and because of the straightness of the tunnel the light was uninterrupted the whole length of 1300 feet. Of course our lamps were extinguished to show this. After gathering a few specimens, which by the kindness of our conductor we were permitted to carry away, we left and after us was closed a strong door over which are the expressive skull and cross bones.

Taking a hack we went back to the Teller House, which we left after dinner, and taking the train down the Zig-Zag proceeded to Forks Creek to go to Georgetown, where we arrived the same evening a little late, a delay having occurred in consequence of the Denver train preceeding having been wrecked by a jackass, who was jack enough to think he could frighten the locomotive by jumping out of the bushes in front of it; the consequence was that both parties came sadly to grief, the locomotive and balance of the train being derailed and badly wrecked and underneath lay silly jack, having made his last bray. The road to Georgetown lays in the gorge and it is still up, up, up to 8,500 feet with the scenery like that already described. We saw mine holes dotting the mountain sides and placer mining going on in the bed of the stream. On our way we pass Idaho Spring, a famous resort on account of the number and variety of mineral springs both hot and cold. One hot spring is of such a temperature that the hand can only be immersed for a moment. These springs are much used by invalids; beyond this attraction, Idaho Springs is but a mining town with nothing peculiar to distinguish it from the others.

Georgetown is fifty miles from Denver, and has a population of 8000, very active as a mining town, and is supplied with the necessary apparatus for reduction of ore, etc. It is in a level basin; the houses are principally of wood. The business of this place is enormous. Far up in the mountains are the Chicago Lakes visited from Georgetown. We did not go to them, but Green Lake, which is more convenient, we concluded to take in. We took passage in a four-horse coach, in which were other tourists, for a three mile ride along and up the mountain sides to an elevation 2000 feet above Georgetown. The incline of the road is fearful (over 600 feet to the mile); the road is one of the roughest, and the precipices terrifying. A broken axle or similar accident on this narrow way, just wide enough for a vehicle, would have precipitated us over the mountain side, and a funeral more or less numerous would have been the inevitable result. In going up the heavy passengers were

placed in the forward part of the coach; coming back was more dangerous, as it was down grade, the heavy members taking the back part, and all holding on to a strong strap extending from end to end to keep them from sliding forward in it. Green Lake is located nearly 11,000 feet above sea level. It is a small but beautiful sheet of the clearest water from the snows on the surrounding and overshadowing mountains, and is skirted by small pine trees. A ride on its placid surface in a row boat enabled us to get a fine view of its beautiful and grand surroundings and also to peer into its depth, which are considerable (several hundred feet). Trunks of trees in various positions are seen at the bottom and they are represented as the remains of a petrified forest. They probably are waterlogged trees from the mountain side. Trout are here by the thousands and are very tame, coming at call to be fed. An old German who seems to attend to this display, has several of them named, being distinguished by size, color or some other distinguishing feature. One is called the Kaiser another Kaiserin, etc., and he speaks tenderly of them, "der arm teufel, er will auch etwas." A convenient building is placed on the edge of the lake for the use of visitors and a hotel is in contemplation.

This getting up in the world will hardly be appreciated by one who has not had the experience, for to speak of ten, eleven, or twelve thousand feet above sea level only conveys the idea of a great height; even two or three thousand feet to one who has never seen it means quite as much. One must stand near a rock and look to its top two or three thousand feet above or be above and look down to know how terrible it is, and how little we are. At no time when we were at our highest elevations were we above all the mountains, there were still those whose sides rose more or less perpendicularly from the roads we were on, not including particular peaks.

Returning to Georgetown without accident, for which we all congratulated ourselves, for the descent was more dangerous than the ascent, we left for Silver Plume, farther up. The road becomes very tortuous and is here known as The Loop, taxing the constructing engineers' resources to their utmost. I cannot describe its windings to be intelligible to another without using a plan, but the following will possibly convey somewhat of an idea: The road passes around the edge of Georgetown and crosses itself by a bridge three hundred feet long and ninety feet high. First you pass under the bridge and proceed up the canon, span Clear Creek and turn again towards Georgetown. From the bridge you look down upon the track below and also upon Georgetown, taking in Devil's Gate and Bridal Veil Falls. Then you turn away from the town, then towards it, and still higher, a complete loop having been made, and three curves, which very nearly become loops. From one point six distinct tracks are visible at different levels, but they are parts that we had passed over, and were parts of our road. At last we reach Silver Plume, 500 feet above Georgetown, less than two miles distant by straight line, but over four and a half by rail.

Silver Plume is a small but busy mining town located in a gulch with but little level ground. The name is derived from a beautiful waterfall in the creek. Mines are on all sides, the dumps from which spread themselves out like fans on the mountain sides. We did not stop but continued on to Graymont, four miles farther on, at the foot of Gray's Peak, from which it derives its name, with bare mountains projecting all around. It was formerly called Bakerville and consists of a new frame hotel of fair size for this place, but of rough construction, a frame house, a log stable, a shingle mill, etc., and is the terminus of the road. It is the resort of visitors and those contemplating an ascent of the peak. We spent the afternoon and night here and had arranged with the liveryman for horses to go up the peak in the morning, but the serious illness of Mrs. B., which came on suddenly, forced us to abandon it and seek a place where, should the illness be protracted, we should have medical service and other comforts. So we left on the first train next day. The high altitude was probably the cause of the illness. Graymont is 2000 feet above Georgetown, eight miles away and nearly 11,000 feet above sea level.

Gray's Peak is 14,441 feet high, the second in height in Colorado, and is called the Dome of the Continent. The ascent is made by carriage to Kelso Cabin, the limit of timber, where the horses are unhitched and saddled, for the carriage road now merges in a narrow trail, which winds around several hills and then goes towards the top by winding round the peak. To go straight up would be impossible. To have failed to reach the peak was to us a great disappointment. The openings of mines are seen all around and it makes one wonder how the miners can get to them or get ore away from them, they seem to be in such inaccessible places. The night spent at Graymont was the most uncomfortable of our trip. Our sense of security was considerably shaken, though probably without cause. The partitions in the hotel were only of boards covered with muslin to conceal the cracks; our next neighbors were somewhat noisy and individuals with dogs in the bar room were apparently up all night, which with loud talking and barking, made us feel uncomfortable in this lonely and elevated part of the country. A huge fire was built outside the house and we did not know how carefully it was managed nor for what purpose it was intended. It was, however, very cold here.

Clear Creek Canon is from end to end a panorama of grandeur and sublimity, with towering walls 3000 feet high in some places. It is a place all tourists should visit. Clear Creek, which plunges through it from its beginning near Graymont to near Denver, with a fall of over 5000 feet is by no means clear. It is at one time crystal waters and milk-white foam, have become muddied of various colors, so to continue while man with pick and drill, penetrates its mountain sides, for all this color is from the washings from stampers and gulches. We return to Denver, leaving behind with regret these wonders to which I have alluded, for a complete description is almost impossible.

Time is flying and there are many miles and many things to claim our attention as we chase the sun towards its setting.

From Denver northward to Cheyenne we pass over the western edge of the desert, with the mountains on the left. We follow the South Platte to within a short distance of Greely, where the river is crossed, and arrive at Cheyenne, one hundred and six miles from Denver, in the evening. The country is flat and only cultivated where irrigation is carried on. Greely is nicely located, has a population of between 3,000 and 4,000, and surrounded by well-kept farms. Cheyenne, in Wyoming Territory, on the main line of the U. P. R. R. five hundred and sixteen miles from Omaha and of 6,038 feet elevation, has a population of six thousand. It is a busy place, beginning originally as a point of distribution to the mining and stock districts of Dakota, Wyoming, Montana, Colorado, etc., which it still is, and besides is an important railroad and stock centre. At Cheyenne we took supper, changed cars and in a sleeper continued our journey towards Ogden. We are still climbing to the backbone of the continent, passing through narrow canons, and curiously-shaped rocks on each side. One in particular near Sherman is called the Hippopotamus Rock, consisting of an irregularly oblong mass representing the body resting upon several smaller ones representing the legs and feet of the ungainly and unwieldy animal after which it has been named. All this is upon an elevated rock platform which resembles huge masonry.

Sherman, thirty-three miles from Cheyenne, at an elevation of 8,235 feet, is reached before dark. It is the highest point of the Union Pacific railroad, and indeed the highest on this transcontinental line. On a sign a short distance from the station are the words, "Summit of the Rocky Mountains." Just beyond Sherman we saw the monument erected to Oakes and Oliver Ames, who were chiefly instrumental in bringing this railroad to completion. It is a pyramid of granite 65 feet high and 60 feet square at the base, and is marked by medallion busts of each of these gentlemen. Dale Creek Bridge, west of Sherman two miles, is built of iron, 600 feet long, over a chasm 130 feet deep. It has rather a delicate appearance, but is a very substantial structure. We enter upon the great Laramie Plains, which are 40 by 100 miles in extent, of fine grazing country, but to the eastern traveler there are here few views except the mountain ranges in the distance which charm the eye. On these plains are pastured many herds of horses, mules and cattle, in numbers that seem almost incredible. These herds do not require shelter and the natural grass is accessible nearly the whole year, there being only a few days each year that it is entirely covered with snow. We also noticed the great number of windmills or rather wind-pumps which supply the water at the railway stations and at other points for cattle and like wants.

Night closes over the scene and we retire, and in the morning look longer for the sun than we did on the eastern slope for we are descending towards the Pacific, though there are steep grades to climb and elevations to be crossed over before we see its waters. The Wind river, Medicine Bow and Snowy ranges of mountains are in the distance and seen from the road, and as we approach Utah the Uintah range comes into view. The country grows more barren and seems to produce nothing but sage brush. The eye tires of it and the attention is turned to other matters such as reading, talking or sleeping, for though crossing the Rocky mountains, you would wonder that they could be so named, for there is not that roughness that you are led to expect. It is the high altitude that we are on, and the proximity of snow-capped mountains which give indication that we are crossing the back-bone of the continent. Sage brush is a small shrub of varying height from six inches to three or four feet, with narrow oval leaves, of a sage-green color, sometimes yellowish and having a slightly aromatic odor. It grows in little bunches, and generally where no timber is to be seen. It is useless except that sheep, deer and antelope feed upon it, because there is nothing else to eat when they are in the sage-brush region.

We pass over gullies and by castellated rocks which stand out alone on the plain or run in ranges of a similar character and are from 300 to 1000 feet high. Snow sheds that are continuous for miles and resemble tunnels lined with timbers, there being at regular intervals apertures for the admission of light; sometimes they stand out clear, at others they are built against the mountain side with timbers, one would suppose equal to any force which could be applied to them, but they are often carried away bodily. Fire trains are kept at various points loaded with water tanks, hose, etc., to be conveyed to any point where the sheds may be attacked by the devouring element. Great care is required for under the summer's sun and no rain for weeks, these sheds become dried and are almost like tinder in their tendency to inflame. Snow fences are also numerous and continuous. They are made of light material with the rails or cross-pieces not very close together, and at certain points consist of several parallel lines from 50 to 100 feet apart. These break the force of the wind when driving the snow and force the latter to drift near the fences and keep it from the track, at least very materially reducing the quantity. From what we have observed at this season of the year, we would hesitate to cross these wastes in winter, and if we did we would provide ourselves with considerable provision, for sometimes trains are snow bound for days and no eating stations for miles and no means of getting to them. It is related that in the winter of 1871 and 1872 there was a seventeen days snow blockade and deep enough to bury the standing telegraph poles.

Besides the stations, which are generally most insignificant, often consisting of not more than two or three houses and very often often of only a side track, we saw what are known as "dug-outs" in which live miners, herdsmen and even families. They are built by digging out a cellar, raising a low side wall of turf covered with timber and earth. They are sometimes very capacious for that kind of building and very comfortable, for they are almost impervious to cold and are in little danger of collapse from the fierce winds which sweep these heights. Sod houses are also made where that material can be obtained, and are comfortable, that is, for this section. They would be regarded in the east as scarcely fit for beasts.

Creston, seven hundred and thirty-eight miles from Omaha and 7,030 feet above sea level, is so called because it is near the divide. It consists of a telegraph station, side tracks and a section house. Three miles west is the summit or divide, from which the waters pass to the east and west respectively, though this place is 1122 feet lower than Sherman. Here is desolation; there seems to be no living thing, animal or vegetable. The elements have here free play and appear to do so to the detriment of everything, even the ground over which they move. The view a short distance from here is one of the most extensive in this section and is estimated at about two hundred miles. This is the "Continental Divide."

We pass on over alkali plains upon which nothing grows. The dust enters the cars to the great annoyance of eyes and nose, for it is very irritant. Bitter Creek, which passes through a valley of the same name, is so called because its water is impregnated with alkali, which renders it almost useless. Some of the scenery in this valley reminds us of some in Colorado, only they are not so great. The country for miles each way is underlaid with coal, the seams coming to the surface very frequently; it is of good quality and easily mined. Rock Springs, eight hundred and thirty-one miles from Omaha, is the great coal depot on the Union Pacific Railroad, and is a great distributing point of this great necessity, which is said to be of superior quality, second only to anthracite; it is called "lignite."

We next come to Green River Valley through which passes Green River. Green River station is a dining station, and when the surrounding country is taken into consideration, one would naturally expect that provisions, etc., would be scarce, and the prospect of a square meal would be very scanty, but I assure you an agreeable surprise awaits all who try the fare. This and other eating stations along the road are owned and managed by the railroad company, and they make elegant and liberal provision. This is necessary in a desert country like this, and dining cars are not on all trains. Almost all the provisions have to be brought to these places from more or less remote points on the road, and it is to the interest of the company that they should be good and in plenty and not extravagant in price.

The Green River Valley is curious and interesting. It abounds with fossils and moss agates, but is otherwise barren. Stratified rocks of strange shapes and great size abound, with impressions of fossil-fish, plants and insects at every cleavage. The Twin Sisters, two masses of rock, probably 200 feet high and 50 feet at the base, standing alone on a little knoll; Castle Rock, high up on a bluff, resembling the tower of a castle; Giant's Club, 250 feet high, standing alone with almost perpendicular sides, is club-shaped and is smaller towards the base than at the top, and is likened to a club with its handle stuck in the ground. The Giant's Teapot is of the same material as the club, but not by any means so high. It stands on a knoll and resembles the old-fashioned four sided China teapot, having a projection like a spout but no handle. Green River Valley is surrounded by bluffs of the same material as the rocks just mentioned. The road follows one side at a considerable elevation above the river's bed. It was once a lake of considerable dimensions and the whole area shows evidence of water washings.

Red Canon is passed through, with sides rising to a height of 3000 feet and very grand. We now enter the valley of Black's Fork, which is located in the Uintah mountains and is full of beautiful scenery, cones, and buttes variously named arising on all sides, which, under the influence of the elements, are gradually melting away. The site of Bear River City is passed, and the only evidences of a once lively town, founded in 1868, are the head-boards of graves containing the bodies of some of its early but very rough settlers. At Evanstown, nine hundred and fifty-seven miles from Omaha, we find a small but flourishing town, having a round-house, car and machine shops, with coal and lumber interests of considerable magnitude. It has also an eating station where elegant meals are served to travellers, Chinese waiters in their native costumes waiting upon the tables. There is quite a community here of these Chinese and their quarter is called Chinatown, where they have their Joss House and other buildings peculiar to these people.

From here westward we get among the Mormons. They are principally farmers in this vicinity and are to be found in all directions, from one to two hundred miles north, east, south, and west of Salt Lake City. We leave Wyoming and at Wahsatch we are at the approach to the famous Echo Canon in Utah. This canon is full of wonders. Cathedral and Castle Rocks, hundreds of feet high, and alongside of which ordinary habitations are but ant hills; Hanging Rock projecting many feet from the mass to which it is attached and threatening to fall; Sentinel Rock standing erect and alone on a bluff as a sentinel on duty; Witch's Rocks and Bottles, turreted and flask like; Egyptian Tombs, resembling at first sight the exteriors of those wonderful excavated rock tombs found along the Nile in Egypt; Pulpit Rock high above Echo Creek, which resembles a pulpit, and it is traditionally said that sermons have been delivered from it (perhaps they were "sermons in stones"); Monument Rock, standing like a high, time-worn and lightning-shattered obelisk, marking an epoch in the earth's pre-historic existence. These are but a part of the many curious forms, and convey but little idea of the ruggedness and grandeur of this canon, with its red sandstone and conglomerate walls, cliffs, and ledges, from a few hundred to a thousand feet high. In this canon we pass a number of stations and small towns, but they are insignificant and of no interest.

From Echo Canon we pass on and enter Weber Canon, traversed by Weber river. The rocks are dark gray and present somewhat different features from those of Echo. The mountains on each side, while very high, do not have nearly such perpendicular faces. The Thousand Mile Tree is here with a sign hanging to it indicating the fact; it is one thousand miles from Omaha. Now this tree has nothing to boast of except that it occupies this place and is the largest of any of the trees in the neighborhood, and that is saying very little for it. It stands alone near the track and is always noticed by the passengers in the trains.

The Devil's Slide, a short distance from the Thousand Mile Tree, and on the opposite side of the canon, is made up of two perpendicular and parallel masses of granite, projecting a number of feet above the surface level of the side of the mountain to which they are attached. They are about fourteen feet apart, and eight hundred feet long, and extend from near the top of the mountain to the edge of the river; the space between the walls constitutes the slide. It is a very rough slide and it is not known whether his satanic majesty turned eastward or westward when he arrived at the bottom. We think, however, that he devoted considerable time to the east, and when Mexico turned this country over to Uncle Sam he hied himself back towards the Pacific. The early history of the west points conclusively to such an action. He has stopped sliding, however, unless in some of the wild storms and in the dead of night he indulges in this pastime, as Hendrick Hudson and his crew, covered with bar-

nacles and sea weeds, amused themselves in rolling ten pins in the Catskills when wind and rain were most furious, thunder the loudest and lightning the brightest; and if you don't believe it go and hear what Joe Jefferson says about Rip Van Winkle. As the slide still remains I think he must be not far away, and besides, Devil's Gate must be passed through before we can reach Ogden. It is just beyond and is a rough and rugged opening in the mountain; the pass to which it leads is very grand. The old wagon road used in the overland transit is seen cut from the solid rock, for there is no other level space over which wagons could be drawn.

Before entering Devil's Gate we were shown, far off in the mountain top, holes in the rocks, which projected. They appeared no larger than a hat yet we were assured they were several feet in diameter. They are said to have been caused by the winds, but for this we cannot vouch. The light is seen passing through them, which proves them to be complete perforations. Leaving Weber Canon we passed over a number of bridges and through tunnels. We are ushered into the Great Salt Lake Basin, once covered by water, afterward a desert, but by man converted into a fertile and productive country, a condition which might be brought about in many parts of the desolate and barren country through which we have passed. Artesian wells are bored here and there for the convenience of the railroad company, but more of these, with their water conducted over the land would enable it to be cultivated with profit. In all probability this will be done, as also the utilizing of streams, which now only follow their beds, but by dams, pumps and flumes, they may be made to serve man's purpose to his comfort and profit and make the country useful and beautiful.

Following the Weber River we arrive at Ogden early in the evening, having been twenty-four hours on the rail. Here we took supper and at 7 p. m. left for Salt Lake City, where we arrived an hour later, and stopped at the Continental Hotel. Early to bed for good rest we arose in the morning refreshed, and immediately got ready to do this most wonderful of the western cities, founded under most peculiar circumstances and prospering under influences regarded to be most demoralizing. Here is the centre of the Mormon world. This city lies upon a plain in the valley of the Jordan River (which is part of the Great Salt Lake Basin) having the Wahsatch mountains rising on the east and just behind it, with the river on the west. This is an oasis in the desert and was commenced in July, 1847, by the Mormons from Missouri, under the leadership of Brigham Young. The city is laid out in rectangular plots of ten acres each, with wide streets, having long rows of shade trees growing at their curbs. The buildings range from most imposing stone structures used for public and business purposes, to dwellings of stone and wood more or less pretentious; the hotels are large, convenient and well kept, and the visitor is immediately struck with the great cleanliness and general good order of the place whichever way considered. The modern conveniences of water works, gas works, hotel elevators, etc., which are regarded as indispensable in these days, are here adopted in the most approved style. The city government is in the same general form as that of other cities of the same class.

Armed with letters of introduction we sallied forth to see the city. We first stopped at the county court house to find the U. S. Surrogate Judge, and failing in this we were referred to the U. S. Court. In going there we came upon ex-judge Smith of the Municipal Court. He is an elderly man, using crutches and is a first cousin of the original Joseph Smith, of Nauvoo fame, and founder of Mormonism. We also met Mr. Cannon, brother of Geo. Q. Cannon, who was sent to Congress as representative of the territory in that body, but was rejected because he had three wives. We had a very pleasant talk with these and other dignitaries of the church and from them we obtained considerable information; their courtesy will be long remembered. We had been informed that Mormons could be identified as such anywhere, particularly the females; but we saw nothing to indicate a distinguishing feature from Catholic, Episcopalian or other sect, and to this our newly made acquaintances rather humorously alluded. We had also been told that the hatred of the Mormons for the Gentiles was such that the churches, halls, etc., of other than the Mormon denomination were broken into and their windows and interiors destroyed by them, and the inmates interfered with. Our new friends called attention to the churches in view from where we were talking and we did not see anything but evidences of peace and good order. Personal violence in the direction of persecution was in no wise indicated, but these gentlemen when asked whether other than Mormons could purchase property and obtain clear titles, said that they could, but that where there were two applicants, one a Mormon the other a Gentile, the former would receive the pref-

erence, for they knew what kind of a neighbor he would be and how far to depend on him in the administration of municipal affairs. We were kindly directed as to objects of interest, even giving us assistance by personal attention. Others to whom we were not introduced were not less kind, not saying, "Go this way or that," but "Come this way and I will show you." These volunteered attentions stamp these people as among the most courteous to strangers that we have ever met.

The Tabernacle would be a wonder in any part of the country, but here it is more wonderful, when the disadvantages of time and place of building are considered. It is unlike any other building in the United States so far as we know. It is like a large inverted oval basin supported on forty-four sandstone pillars, three by nine feet in size and from fourteen to twenty feet high. The building is two hundred and fifty feet long, one hundred and fifty feet wide and seventy feet from the floor to the highest part of the ceiling; the roof is ten feet higher. This immense dome is said to be the largest self supporting arch in America, with one exception. There are no pillars except those which support the whole at the edge. A gallery extends around three sides of the interior and is thirty feet wide. The seats are not upholstered and arranged as in churches generally; the pulpit is placed at some distance from one end, so as to enable all to hear the speaker; behind this is the organ, the largest on the western slope, requiring four blowers, and is said to be very fine. The seating capacity is ten thousand with standing room for several thousand more. The immense ceiling is festooned throughout with evergreens, and presents a very attractive appearance. The accoustic properties of this building are remarkable. From the pulpit a speaker in an ordinary tone of voice, even in a whisper, can be heard in any part of the building, and better far away than very near to the speaker. A pin (not a spike) dropped into a hat upon the pulpit can also be heard. These points were demonstrated to us by the kindness of our conductor. In this building are held the Sunday services in summer, but as there are no provisions for heating, services in winter are held in an adjoining building. The Tabernacle is built almost entirely of native material, even to the furniture and organ, the shingles on the roof also having been made in Salt Lake City. It is enclosed by a high wall made of cobble or round river stones and mortar. The New Temple on the same block and within the same enclosure as the Tabernacle, is an imposing building of granite, smooth dressed, one hundred and eighty-six and a half feet north and south and ninety-nine feet east and west; the walls are seven and eight feet thick and very durable. This building was commenced in 1853 and is still incomplete.

The Edowment house is a large building in the Tabernacle enclosure in which marriages are consecrated, and the people both men and women, undergo certain secret ceremonial services by which they become sealed to each other or to Heaven. The performances in this place have been regarded by some as barbarous and grossly indelicate, but of this we cannot say. The Tithing House in the same enclosure, is the depository of tithes paid by the Mormons for the benefit of the church, and consist of money, merchandize, grain, cattle and other products; those who have not material tithes to contribute give an equiva'ent in labor. The articles thus collected are either given in payment to those employed to do any work for the church, or they are converted into money, and that is used to pay; and it is also dispensed in charity, for this church organization is a large and powerful corporation with many enterprises other than religious religious, and beggary is not permitted.

The residence of Brigham Young is quite imposing. Here he lived, had his offices, gave his orders and received visitors, and those having business with him. Adjoining is a row of houses in which he kept his numerous wives. Amelia Palace, a fine building, was erected for his principal wife, Amelia, but he did not live to see it completed. We visited these places. Brigham Young died August 29th, 1877, and is buried on his place near by, which is reached by passing through the Eagle Gateway, the arch of which extended over the street and was surmounted by an eagle. The arch is now, down, but the stone pillars which supported it still remain. The ground where he is laid contains his vault, cut out of solid granite, and the slab covering his body is bolted down. Around this spot is an ornamental iron fence six feet high; the whole plot is surrounded by a wall eighteen inches high surmounted by an iron fence four feet high. This is the shrine which all good Mormons visit; 'tis the Mormon Kaba and Salt Lake City is the Mormon Mecca. Other buildings as Social Hall, Salt Lake Theatre, City Hall, Council House, hotels, churches of various religious denominations, etc., are of very substantial construction and some of them are of fine architecture.

Z. M. C. I, Zion's Mutual Co-operative Institution, under the control of the chief Mormon officers, combines the manufacture, purchase and sale of nearly all articles necessary for the people; branch houses are to be found in all of the larger Mormon towns. The building in Salt Lake City is very large and is known as the "Big Co'op." It is well stored with goods. At this time an inventory of stock was being taken and the doors were closed to all comers. The motto of this institution is "Holiness to the Lord," derived from the Bible and supposed to have a specific meaning here. Business is also carried on by others than Mormons, but Mormons prefer to patronize those of their own faith.

About three miles east of the city on the Wahsatch mountains is Camp or Fort Douglass, overlooking the city. This belongs to and is garrisoned by the United States. We did not visit it though courteously invited to do so by an officer whom we met. With Mr. Werner, United States Surrogate Judge, we made a call upon the governor of Utah. This position was formerly filled by Brigham Young. Desirous of knowing more of the Mormons than we could learn in the east, we made a visit to the Deseret Publishing Company and purchased the Book of Mormon (which is the Mormon Bible) and sundry other works containing the Articles of Faith, etc. With minds more or less prejudiced against the Mormons we were quite discomfitted on finding their apparent frankness, extreme affability, and earnest endeavor to correct what they claim to be false statement as to their government, their creed and their treatment of Gentiles. A short synopsis of their history may not be uninteresting.

Joseph Smith the founder and known as "The Prophet" was born in Vermont in December, 1805. His father was a farmer and able to give his son only a meagre common school education. When ten years old his parents removed to Palmyra, New York. The religious influence surrounding him was of the Presbyterian creed. When about fifteen years old, being dissatisfied with the doctrines of this and other denominations, he was prompted by a scripture text to seek the Lord in his own way, so retiring to a grove he commenced praying and then had a vision of two angels who assured him his sins were forgiven and that the different denominations were not acknowledged of God as His church and kingdom, but that in the fullness of time he should receive the true creed. Telling his experience to others he was by them subjected to persecution which continued. In 1823 he had another vision and visitation by a bright angel setting forth that the time was approaching for the gospel to be preached preparatory to the second coming of the Messiah, and that he was the chosen one to bring about some of the purposes of this dispensation. He was also informed that certain records of the ancient Hebrew prophets were concealed, but that by God's direction he should discover them. The vision was twice renewed that same night and also the next day while in the field. He immediately started to the spot where the angel said these records were, which spot he immediately recognized near Manchester, Ontario county, N. Y. Here he found certain metallic plates variously inscribed in an unknown tongue with a key to decipher the same. He did not remove them until four years subsequently, as he was ordered by the angel. The plates constituted the original Book of Mormon. After he had obtained them, the persecution waxed stronged, so that his life was in danger. In consequence of this he left for Pennsylvania, packing the plates in a barrel of beans to preserve them from seizure, for an endeavor had been made to take them, and in this State he commenced his translation of them which was published in 1830; this edition is scarce and costly. The translation of the title of the book as taken from the plate having equivalent characters is as follows, "The Book of Mormon, an Account Written by the hand of Mormon, upon Plates, taken from the Plates of Nephi."

He continued to have visions and visitations, and having a few who believed in his special election to serve God's purposes, they organized the "Church of Jesus Christ of Latter Day Saints." Persecutions by mobs and individuals continued and they went to Kirtland, Ohio, and subsequently to Missouri and Illinois, establishing on the prairies a number of thriving settlements. Everywhere they were the recipients of the same attentions that they received in New York, causing their migration. Growing in power and wealth, their influence was wanted in politics, which the political parties failed to obtain. Soldiers were even arrayed against them and many were arrested; others were shot down in the streets. Joseph Smith was taken from jail in Carthage, Illinois, and murdered by the soldiery, June 27, 1844. Martyrdom in time past was horrible, but that such should be in the United States in the nineteenth century is certainly a blot upon our history. This martyrdom of Jos. Smith seems to have been hallowed by the divine presence if the statements relative thereto are correct. Hyrum Smith, an elder brother of Joseph, was also murdered in the Carthage jail on the same date.

The Saints selected Brigham Young, an apostle, as successor to Smith in the presidency of the organization. They settled in the western part of Missouri in some three or four counties, north, east, and south of where Kansas City now stands. Here, just as they thought themselves secure, the spirit of intolerance arose and they were actually given notice to leave the country under penalty of destruction of property and life. Brigham Young conceived the idea of going toward the Pacific Ocean with his people, where in territory not under the dominion of the United States he would establish a new Jerusalem for his people, where they might organize and worship God without hindrance.

Brigham Young was a Yankee of the Methodist denomination. He was a man of extraordinary power, which he wielded over his willing subjects; his management and foresight were marvellous. Polygamy had been secretly introduced after the patriarchal manner, and though not kindly received by all, was said to be necessary to please God; besides as all new organizations and colonies get a vast deal of their strength from the young, the begetting of children was ingeniously made a religious obligation, and its failure was a sore trial to the deluded men and woman who believed that their position in heaven depended upon their obedience of the command, "Be fruitful and multiply."

The western states, into which the Mormons first emigrated, were but thinly settled. Illinois was but a young state, and Missouri was on the frontier. In these two states numerous persons resided whose presence in the east had become intolerable by violation of the laws or other reprehensible acts, and they preferred to take up new quarters at points more or less remote from the scenes of their offences and escape the punishment they merited. Many of these allied themselves with the new organization, probably on account of its novelty or to more thoroughly conceal their identity, contributing very materially to its success prior to and during the exodus to the Pacific slope. They were courageous, daring, loved adventure, cared not for hardship, and a better opportunity for demonstration could not have offered.

Brigham Young managed these with a firmness amounting almost to military discipline and with a success which must command respect and excite astonishment. Without any definite place in view, but with faces turned toward the setting sun, Brigham Young at the head of one hundred and forty-three persons and a wagon train, set out from Independence, Missouri, and adjacent places and proceeded over the plains which were known only to hunters, traders and Indians, and part of which was an almost trackless desert. This was April 14, 1847. This band experienced trials in this expedition which would be horrible to relate; hunger and thirst affecting both human and brute; Indi ns, when not on the war path, harrassed them by their thieving disposition; untravelled passes in the Rocky Mountains, narrow and dangerous trails made by man or animals, a journey probably more extensive than that of the forty years wandering of the Israelites in the Desert of Sinai after the Egyptian captivity, and probably fuller of adventure and suffering. But with an object in view, fostered with a belie. in a divine mission, these people murmured but little, if at all, and when they came within a few days march of where Salt Lake City is now located, a small and trusty band was sent ahead, who like Caleb and Joshua of old, were to spy out the land and make early report.

On the 22d of July, Orson Pratt and the small company of which he was the head from the mountains discovered the valley where they subsequently settled. After riding through it they returned and reported to the main body. Two days later the whole party entered the valley with praise and thanksgiving to God, for here they saw the promised land. Dire must have been their distress that they should have been thus gladdened at this time; the land did not bear grapes of great size, for there were no vines, nor did the land flow with milk and honey for there were neither cattle, flowers nor bees. The land was gently sloping toward a river in the valley, the valley several miles in width and surrounded by high mountains. The land was a barren waste, it was a desert without shrub or blade of grass, but multitudes of large black bugs had possession of the place. However they felt themselves beyond the reach of their persecutors and they were happy.

On the 28th of July they laid off the plan of the present city of Salt Lake, two miles square, with streets eight rods wide and blocks of ten acres each, the lines running due east and west, north and south. This they called "Zion" and proceeded to erect such shelter as they could, adopted some means of defence against the Indians, and settled down to stay. They prepared the ground and planted seed which they had brought with them, and by irrigation they eventually got a good crop. A large number, among them Brigham Young, retraced their steps to

Missouri to bear glad tidings of the New Canaan to their families and friends, and take them there, where they arrived the last of October, 1847, having much of the same experiences of the first expedition, except that the way was known, and places of extreme difficulty avoided where possible. Brigham Young returned to Salt Lake the next year, with the remainder of the people and such others as had recently adopted their faith and cast their lot amongst them, when all went actively to work to build and cultivate. The blocks of ten acres each constituted wards, to each of which was assigned an elder who became the guardian of and accountable for all which transpired upon it, making daily reports to headquarters. A temporary tabernacle had been erected for worship. In order to extend the influence and power of the organization settlements were established in adjacent parts of the country, but all tributary to the central power at Salt Lake City. Brigham Young apparently designed establishing a Mormon kingdom.

When Brigham Young took possession of the country "in the name of the Lord" the country belonged to Mexico, but in March, 1848, the territory which includes almost all the present states and territories from the Rocky mountains to the Pacific Ocean, was ceded to the United States. He, however, paid no attention to this, and in March, 1849, the Saints met in convention and organized "A free and independent government by the name of the state of Deseret." This included nearly all the territory west of the Rockies. Brigham Young soon after sent a delegate to Washington avowedly to open negotiations looking to the admission of Deseret into the Union; but the tone he assumed, we learn, was as that of a representative of a foreign power demanding recognition. To this Congress paid no attention, but in 1850 organized the present territory of Utah, making Brigham Young governor, and it is stated that up to the day of his death, the State of Deseret existed de facto, and he its governor, and that the said state exists in spite of the territorial organization; that Brigham Young as its governor convened its Legislature of thirty-nine Mormon high priests, the same composing the Utah Legislature and which was convened immediately after the latter's adjournment. The saints adopted the policy of seclusion and termed all others than Mormons as Gentiles, and regarded them with the same distrust and hatred as the Jews did the Gentiles of old.

The gold discovery of California eventually brought miners and others among them, very much to their disgust. They have been growing and extending their power, and that outrages occurred there can be no doubt; also flagrant violations of the laws and customs of our country; yet they have grown in strength and grandeur, and present the appearance of being law-abiding, which one might wish was more regarded in the east. Brigham Young was born in Vermont, June 1st, 1801, was received into the church of the Latter Day Saints, April 14th, 1832; was elected one of the twelve apostles, February 14th, 1835; led the first pioneer journey to Salt Lake, April 14th, 1847; led the final journey of the Saints to Salt Lake, May 26th, 1848, with 1,891 persons and over six hundred wagons, occupying four months in the trip. He was elected president of the church December 24th, 1847; was elected governor of the state of Deseret, March 9th, 1849; appointed by the United States, governor of Utah and superintendent of Indian affairs, September 30th, 1850, which he held nearly eight years. He continued president of the church and governor of Deseret until his death, August 29th, 1877. He left seventeen wives, sixteen sons and twenty-eight daughters, and was the father of fifty-eight children. He was a man who weighed nearly two hundred pounds, had a large head, high forehead, was large featured and showed great firmness and determination, which latter characteristics stamps him as one of the remarkable men of his age and without which there probably would have been rebellion, and certainly Salt Lake City would have been nothing as compared with its present condition.

For the better understanding I will here insert the "Articles of Faith, of the Church of Jesus Christ of Latter Day Saints."

1. We believe in God the Eternal Father, and in his son Jesus Christ, and in the Holy Ghost.

2. We believe that men will be punished for their own sins, and not for Adam's transgression.

3. We believe that through the atonement of Christ, all mankind may be saved, by obedience to the laws and ordinances of the Gospel.

4. We believe that these ordinances are: First, faith in the Lord Jesus Christ; second, repentance; third, baptism by immersion for the remission of sins; fourth, laying on of hands for the gift of the Holy Ghost.

5. We believe that a man must be called of God by "prophecy and by the laying on of hands," by those who are in authority, to preach the Gospel and administer the ordinances thereof.

6. We believe in the same organization that existed in the primitive church, viz: apostles, prophets, pastors, teachers, evangelists, etc., etc.

7. We believe in the gift of tongues, prophecy, revelation, visions, healing, interpretation of tongues, etc.

8. We believe the Bible to be the Word of God, as far as it is translated correctly. We also believe the Book of Mormon to be the Word of God.

9. We believe all that God has revealed and all that He does now reveal, and we believe that He will yet reveal many great and important things pertaining to the Kingdom of God.

10. We believe in the literal gathering of Israel, and in the restoration of the Ten Tribes. That Zion will be built upon this continent. That Christ will reign personally upon the earth, and that the earth will be renewed and receive its paradisical glory.

11. We claim the privilege of worshipping Almighty God according to the dictates of our conscience, and allow all men the same privilege, let them worship how, where or what they may.

12. We believe in being subject to kings, presidents, rulers and magistrates, in obeying, honoring and sustaining the law.

13. We believe in being honest, true, chaste, benevolent, virtuous, and in doing good to *all men*; indeed we may say that we follow the admonition of Paul, "We believe all things, we hope all things," we have endured many things and hope to be able to endure all things. If there is anything virtuous, lovely or of good report or praiseworthy, we seek after these things.   JOSEPH SMITH.

It will be seen that the Mormons accept the Bible and New Testament as meaning exactly what they say; they believe in the divinity of Christ, his crucifixion to redeem the wicked world, the necessity of repentance to gain pardon for sin, the holy communion, baptism, and in fact all that is regarded as necessary by the most orthodox denomination. How well they live up to the articles of their faith we cannot tell; by the whole country they are regarded as monsters of iniquity.

They have also adopted the Book of Mormon as second only to the Bible. It is represented as a translation of the plates found by Joseph Smith, being an account of the actions of God among the aborigines of America who were the descendants of the ten tribes of Israel. The characters on the plates were said to be reformed Egyptian and a Urim and Thumim or key found with the plates was used to decipher them. The whole, that is, the the preparation of the plates, was by inspiration, their concealment was by divine command, their discovery and translation was by divine order and revelation to Joseph Smith, who was the ordained instrument of God to accomplish this work and disseminate the same among all people. The plates were said to have been buried 1400 years. An inquiry by us as to where they now are elicited the answer that, the angel took them away. We believed just so much as we pleased and our readers may do the same. The Book of Mormon is written in the style of Chronicles of the Bible, and is a curious production.

The Mormons have adopted a high priesthood of the orders of Aaron and Melchizedek; also apostles, elders, priests, deacons, etc., with particular duties both religious and secular. The intricacies of polygamic faith, the sealing of women to men both dead and alive, the ceremonies of the endowment house, are such that time only could discover them to the uninitiated and we do not intend to dwell upon them here. Polygamy is, however, one of the points which excite the country against them, though, if they maintain their wives as they represent they do, and do not tolerate adultery and fornication, they certainly are not so much to be condemned. We do not wish to be regarded as their advocates, but state the conditions as we learned them, and our impressions in consequence.

This synopsis of history and creed is derived principally from books, etc., which we obtained in Salt Lake City and from conversations with people there, coupled with our own recollections of the excitement and reports respecting the Mormons more than forty years ago. They have made the land grow grapes and literally flow with milk and honey; they have a land which, when the broad fields of grain are viewed, also numerous herds of cattle, etc., etc., suggestive of comfort and prosperity, will make many envious of them. Missionaries are in various parts of the world, as America, Europe and even Australia preaching the doctrines of Mormonism and inviting proselytes to the Zion in the Desert beside the waters of the Jordan, which efforts are not wholly fruitless. John Taylor succeeded Brigham Young in the presidency of the church and still remains so.

Before leaving Salt Lake City we took a ride to the Great Salt Lake, twenty miles distant by rail. This is the most remarkable body of salt water yet discovered. It is eighty miles long, fifty miles wide, and of great depth. It is interspersed with islands and mountains of considerable height. It is surrounded by the Wahsatch and Oquirrh ranges, and is 4,200 feet above the ocean. The saltness

of this lake is remarkable, being about 24 per cent. of salt, and it is related that a few years ago it was 33 per cent. Even now the shrubs adjacent to the lake become covered with the crystalized salt from the evaporated water dashed on them in spray. We obtained at the lake one beautiful and white specimen two and a half inches thick with a small twig in the centre. The lake has no outlet and is supplied by numerous small rivers. The evaporation is becoming less each year as the rainfall increases, and the time is looked for when it will overrun its banks and become less salt. The saltness is ascribed to salt springs in its bottom, also percolation from the salt plains which abound in this territory. Salt plains are not confined to Utah, for we have seen a report of a railroad in southern Colorado which is ballasted with rock salt dug out in grading the road bed. The salt and alkali plains of this section will become more and more deprived of their saline constituents as the rainfall increases and make the land more suitable for cultivation.

The Great Salt Lake is a great resort for tourists and residents of Salt Lake who go to bathe in its invigorating waters, which are so buoyant that one cannot sink in them. We took a bath and were both surprised and delighted. After spending a few hours here we took the train and returned to Salt Lake City, which we left the same afternoon, carrying pleasant recollections of our visit and regrets that we could not make a longer stay in this region. We arrived at Ogden, took supper and changed to cars on the Central Pacific Railroad. Ogden is a Mormon town of great importance as a railroad point and is the connecting point of the U. P. R. R. and the C. P. R. R; also the starting point of the Utah Central and Utah Northern railroad. It is located on the Weber River, a short distance from the Great Salt Lake. It is provided with car and repair shops and many other buildings; iron, coal, and other valuable minerals abound in the vicinity, making it probable that this will become a manufacturing place. The town is regularly laid out upon two levels, constituting an upper and lower town, the upper part having principally the private residences, the lower town being the business part. The Mormons have a temple and other denominations their churches. Water runs through the streets, as is the case in all these Rocky mountain towns, mountain streams supplying the water. By this means trees are cultivated and gardens planted with grass and flowers.

After supper we entered a sleeper and then started again toward the Golden

Gate. We pass Corrinne, 809 miles from San Francisco, the most important Gentile town in the territory. At 780 miles from San Francisco we reach Promontory which is now of only historic importance. Here the "Great Railroad Wedding" took place, which joined the U. P. and C. P. railroads and made the trans continental line complete; here the last spike was driven 1085.8 miles from Omaha, May 10, 1869. The ceremonies were grand and impressive. Locomotives with trains of invited guests approached each other from each side of the road and when the last spike was driven the forward ones approached until their pilots touched and persons standing on them reached out and shook hands, pouring libations of wine upon the track and drinking to the success of the enterprise. Telegraphic operators were at the keys to announce the instant of completion, and at 2:47 p. m., Promontory Point gave signal to the rest of the world, waiting anxiously for the word, "DONE," followed by the official announcement:

"PROMONTORY SUMMIT, UTAH, "MAY, 10th. THE LAST RAIL IS LAID! "THE LAST SPIKE IS DRIVEN! THE PA- "CIFIC RAILROAD IS COMPLETED. THE "POINT OF JUNCTION IS 1086 MILES WEST "OF THE MISSOURI RIVER, AND 690 MILES "EAST OF SACRAMENTO CITY.

"LELAND STANFORD, "CENTRAL PACIFIC R. R.

"T. C. DURANT, }
"SIDNEY DILLON, } UNION PACIFIC R R.
"JOHN DUFF, }

From what has been said of the characteristics of the country we have thus far passed through it can be readily imagined that the building of this road was beset on all sides with natural or other obstacles, but the part comprised in the Central Pacific was attended by extraordinary difficulties and cost. All of the material for construction, as rails, spikes, tools, locomotives and cars, had to be transported from New York across the Isthmus of Panama or go around Cape Horn to reach San Francisco. As the road neared completion ten miles a day were laid, showing the number of hands and the energy displayed. The men who conceived the idea of a trans-continental railway were regarded as lunatics, and with a knowledge of the country through which it passes this belief cannot be regarded as extraordinary; but 'tis now a fixed fact and this wonder of the 19th century shows that the projectors were neither demented nor visionary.

The road follows the northern boundary of Great Salt Lake, and at monument we got a view of it from the train. Passing westward towards Nevada, we course along the upper edge of the desert which is immediately west and south of the Great Salt Lake, and as we approach Tecoma we come upon a pile of stones indicating the Nevada state line.

At Elko, five hundred and fifty-eight miles from San Francisco we took breakfast. This town is of considerable commercial and educational importance, the state university being located here. Numerous hot springs are here and used largely by invalids. One, the "Chicken Soup" spring, yields water which it is said only requires salt, pepper and other seasoning to make the illusion perfect. Could it be the outlet of a cauldron of chicken soup deep down in the bowels of the earth, as it has been said that the oil wells of our own state have tapped a school of pre-historic whales?

Here we strike the Humboldt River and follow it a long distance, going through canons and among mountains, sometimes on the plain with sage brush to vary the monotony. At some of the stations, surrounded by desert, we find small encampments of Shoshone Indians. They come to the stations and beg from the passengers and show their papooses which are bound to boards or bark and are curiosities to travellers who tender them a gratuity for the favor. These Indians apparently do nothing but loaf, beg and gamble.

In due time we reach the Humboldt Desert, a sandy plain of considerable dimensions covered with sage brush. We pass several stations of slight importance and many which are but side tracks and signal points. At Humboldt, four hundred and twenty-three miles from San Francisco we took dinner. This is an oasis in the desert; here will be seen trees, grass, flowers and fountains, which relieve the eyes made weary by many monotonous miles of desert and sage brush for these are the first trees, etc., seen since leaving Ogden. Mountains and alkali plains are on all sides, but by irrigation, this place has been made lovely and adjacent land made productive of superior grain and vegetables. The hotel here is well appointed and the decorations of the grounds are remarkable. With hose the grounds and walks are sprinkled prior to the arrival of the train, and passengers avail themselves of a stroll or a rest beneath the trees and bowers, for there is a liberal allowance of time for meals and rest at these places. Sulphur mines exist near by and the shipments are made from this place, the native sulphur yielding about 75 per cent. pure sulphur.

Lovelock's, three hundred and forty-one miles from San Francisco, is only a side track station, telegraph office, store, post-office and a few other buildings; it is important as a grazing place for cattle and the shipment of large quantities of hay raised in the meadows watered by the spreading out of the Humboldt River. It is said upwards of 400,000 head of cattle and sheep graze on these meadows. Farming is carried on with excellent results where irrigation is introduced.

White Plains, three hundred and thirteen miles from San Francisco, is only a side track and is so called because it is in the midst of a white alkali desert. Here salt in fine division exists upon the surface and extends many miles in all directions, and as this is the lowest point (3,849 feet) on the Central Pacific east of the Sierras, the bottom land is often overflowed in the flood season; and the Humboldt and Carson rivers lose themselves in this sink as it is termed, as there is no visible outlet. They sink into the sand, and the balance is established by evaporation and absorption.

Mirage, three hundred and five miles from San Francisco, is but side track and is only interesting from the fact that here this phenomenon is often noticed when the atmosphere is in proper condition and travellers are generally on the lookout. This curious optical delusion is not infrequent on the desert plains of the west, and even on the fertile prairie, often to temporary satisfaction of the weary horseman or teamster who, hoping for a resting place, is doomed to disappointment on finding it vanish as he approaches.

At Reno, two hundred and ninety-three miles from San Francisco, we take supper. This place is situated in a grazing district and is also the point from which tourists start to visit Lake Tahoe, to the south and Pyramid Lake on the north.

Following the Truckee River we soon reach Verdi, the first station in California, making gradual assent into the Sierra Nevada Mountains. We enter snow sheds at various points, like those we have passed through, also through some tunnels, pass by Donner Lake high up in the mountains, made famous as the place where, in the winter of 1846 and '47, a company of eighty-two emigrants were overtaken by a snow storm and nearly all perished. The account is full of horrible detail, as cannibalism is charged against the survivors.

Summit, near by, is one hundred and ninety-five miles from San Francisco, 7,017 feet above sea level, and is the highest point of the road in these mountains. It is surrounded by mountains several thousand feet higher. A fine hotel graces this place and many tourists stop over here to get views of the magnificent scenery from

adjacent points. The road winds along the mountain sides, showing grand scenes from the snow-crowned mountains above to the river in the valley far below. The road enters American River Canon, far up on its sides. This is one of the finest views on the Central Pacific Railroad, and is truly grand. From the narrow stream at the bottom in its rocky bed, the bare rock sides rise directly, widening out and reaching several thousand feet above the water. To see this canon one cannot retire early, as also to see Cape Horn, a projecting mountain, around which the road passes, the sides of which are so steep that workmen were let down from the top to make foothold for excavations for the road-bed, 2,000 feet above the river. If moonlight, these can be seen and the views are awfully grand; if not, the traveller sleeps, for the train passes these points in the night. It was moonlight when we passed.

The train continues on through Sacramento, the moon was low and we slept, but we stopped here on our return trip. Arriving at Benicia, thirty-three miles from San Francisco, the train leaves terra-firma and bodily runs on the ferry boat "Solano," the largest of her class afloat, but so gradual was this that we did not appreciate but that we had run into a large train yard near the water. A little later on we were enabled to investigate this Leviathan of the western waters. Her length over all is four hundred and twenty-four feet, her extreme width is one hundred and sixteen feet, her draught when loaded is six feet six inches. She has two vertical beam engines with sixty inch cylinders and eleven feet stroke; the two side wheels are thirty feet in diameter, of twenty-four paddles each, each paddle having seventeen feet face; each wheel is operated by its own engine to ensure easier management of the boat. There are four rudders at each end of the boat, eleven and one half feet long and five and one half feet deep. There are four railway tracks on deck which will accommodate forty-eight freight cars and and locomotive or twenty-four passenger cars. Benicia is a town of about 1,500 inhabitants and is famous for a large agricultural implement factory besides other industries; it is an admirable shipping point and it is said that at one time it was the rival of San Francisco but this must have been very early. The waters of the Sacramento and San Joaquin rivers pass by it through the Benicia Strait which our monster boat crossed, and passing the straits of Carquinez and along the eastern shore of San Pablo and San Francisco bays we reach Oakland, where we alight and on one of the largest ferry boats we ever saw, we were transported across the bay and landed in San Francisco at 8 a. m. We immediately went to the Russ Hotel when after a wash, breakfast and rest until afternoon, we started for the post office, took a ride in the cable cars and after supper retired. The next day was Sunday and we went to the Howard street Methodist Episcopal church and heard a delightful sermon by Bishop Fowler who had been a passenger on the train with us. After lunch we took a train for the Cliff House and got our first view of the Pacific Ocean with its thousands of miles of expanse.

San Francisco is situated on the western shore of the bay at the upper end of a narrow peninsula extending between the bay and Pacific Ocean. It is *the* port of entry on the west coast of the United States, and has one of the finest harbors in the world. It was named after San Francisco de Assisi, and was first a Catholic Mission dedicated to the above named padre, and founded October 9th, 1776. With the characteristic sluggishness of the old Spaniards little improvement was made and little known of it until the early part of the present century when foreigners began to arrive in small numbers and the place grew somewhat as well as the neighboring country. But it remained for the period after the cession to the United States and the discovery of gold in 1848 to produce the change, and from a village it has grown to the dimensions of a city of nearly 250,000 inhabitants with all the modern improvements. The buildings for business are large and imposing, substantial and convenient. The hotels are numerous and of great size, notably the Palace Hotel which is the largest in the world. It has four fronts, occupying a whole block and covers two and one-fourth acres, it is one hundred and twenty feet high and has an immense number of bay windows on each side which takes away the impression which its great height and size would otherwise make, it is two hundred and seventy-five by three hundred and fifty feet on the sides, and contains seven hundred and fifty-five rooms for guests alone ; it has an immense court-yard which is covered by a sky light where carriages enter and depart with the visitors and guests of the house. This hotel has a world wide reputation and must be seen to be appreciated. The furniture and other appointments with the accomodations are all upon the same grand scale as the size of the building. The Baldwin, Grand Hotel, and Lick House are marvels of grandeur and size only less than the Palace, while the Russ House is commodious, grand, luxurious, convenient and reasonable, ex-

tending along the front of an entire block, attendants efficient and courteous, not hanging around for "tips" so extensively practiced elsewhere and a bane to hotel life; the policy of the management seems to be to charge its patrons a fair price and pay a fair price to, the servants, and requiring that the former shall be served properly without extra charge. We were surprised and gratified at the moderate rates of charge compared with the accommodations which were equal to the best hotels in Philadelphia and New York. We can recommend the Russ House to the most exacting. The churches are numerous and very fine, all denominations are represented, even to that of the heathen Chinee who has his Joss House. The places of amusement are the Grand Opera House, California Theatre, Baldwin Theatre, Bush Street Theatre, and many others where grand and comic operas are rendered and the legitimate drama and variety performances attract the people. As there is here a large floating population more places of amusement are supported than in most places of equal size. The Post Office and Custom Building and Mint are in keeping with the importance of the place and dignity of the United States. The business and commerce are simply enormous. The trade with the East Indies, China, Japan, Australia, Sandwich Islands, Alaska, Western South America and Mexico, centre at this point, and the forest of masts in the harbor fly the flags of all nations. A visit to the wharves showed them to be most substantial, and extensive, having great docking space and covered in many instances with large buildings for storage and other purposes. The dry and floating docks are very large, capable of receiving the largest vessels which enter the harbor. Who that has read the newspapers for some years back has not read of the "Pacific Mail?" The Pacific Mail Steamship Company which has its headquarters in San Francisco, has a fleet of six first class steamers which go between this port and China, Japan, Sandwich Islands and Australia. We can take a little pride in these vessels as the most if not all of them were built along our own Delaware River. The newspaper notices of the Pacific Mail have been with reference to the stocks, etc., of the company and the various applications to Congress for subsidies. The Oriental and Occidental Steamship Company also send steamers to China and Japan.

Of the different parks the Golden Gate Park is most extensive, it is three and a half miles long and half a mile wide, containing 1,019 acres, much of which has been reclaimed from the sand-hills which are to be found in all directions; the decorations of the grounds, the walks, drives, fountains, lakes, and conservatories are most complete and grand, everything in fact to make it the most elegant place of its kind in the west. We enjoyed our visit to it very much. The Woodward Gardens are almost unique in this country. They resemble the Gardens of Acclimatization in Paris, fine large conservatories, marine and other aquaria, seal tanks, cages of animals and birds, cases of stuffed birds, antiquities, etc., in other words it is a garden of natural sciences. The grounds are beautifully laid out, with asphalt walks, ornamental trees, shrubs, and flower beds, beautiful statuary disposed here and there. An art gallery, music hall, skating rink and restaurant contribute to the entertainment and refreshment of visitors. This little paradise was commenced in 1860 by Mr. R. B. Woodward a gentleman of wealth, (now deceased) who expended vast sums to establish this great and useful attraction to the people of San Francisco. No stranger should miss the opportunity of visiting it while here, as it is easy of access and only a short distance from the centre of the city.

To the visitor the first view of San Francisco from Oakland and the ferry boat is peculiar and surprising; here and there are lofty eminences with buildings upon them and upon landing it is observed that some of the streets continue directly up their sides to the tops, the grade being such that horses with vehicles can scarcely ascend. These eminences are sand-hills and are covered with some of the finest private residences in the city. The difficulties of approach are however reduced to a minimum since the cable cars have been introduced and among the most interesting street sights to the stranger is to see the cars ascending and descending the grades, one car acting as a counter balance to the other and as these roads continue over the hills they are much patronized and develop the country beyond. The cable roads are very extensively used, the cars are most substantially constructed and are the most comfortable of all the public conveyances, being spacious and exceedingly clean. The five cable lines extend for many miles over the city and suburbs and constitute the most admirable system we ever saw and this is the testimony of all visitors. In the northern part of the city is Telegraph Hill which is very steep and reached by cable cars. A view from here is extensive. The city below, the bay on the east, the Gold Horn on the north, and sand-hills and Pacific Ocean on the west. A pavilion for refreshments is at the top which makes it an objective point of an afternoon or evening, and see the ships going out and coming in, and the setting sun. Don't miss it!

Of the streets of San Francisco the citizens are justly proud. They are wide, well paved and very clean; the winds, which are important means of keeping them clean, also contribute from time to time to making them dirty by the fine sand which they carry from the outside of the city and deposit over everything; and who has not heard of the "sand lots" and "Dennis Kearney" the sand lot orator, that fomenter of discord, riot and rebellion, with their consequences, fire, murder and robbery? Happily his socialistic and communistic sentiments are little encouraged. Kearney and his "sand lots" are part of this city.

What will surprise the visitor among the many things new and strange will be to learn if he does not see, that many of the private residences, and among them the most palatial and costly, are but wooden buildings. One reason has been assigned for this that, earthquake shocks are frequently felt but rarely of any severity, and if these buildings were of brick or stone they would more readily tumble down, but as the buildings for business are of brick, stone, or iron, the earthquake excuse cannot apply. A fire among these wooden buildings would be most disastrous.

By cable car we visited Laurel Hill cemetery, perhaps one of the finest here, elegantly laid out and decorated with many monumental works of art and less pretentious markings of the resting places of the dead. A trip to the Cliff House should never be missed, as the view is almost unique. It is situated on a cliff on Point Lobos, on the southern side of the Pacific entrance to the Golden Gate, and is seven miles from San Francisco. It is reached by a steam railway. This house has a broad veranda overlooking the Pacific Ocean on the west. It is a great resort for the people of San Francisco, who, besides taking the fresh breezes from the ocean, also are interested in observing the seals which climb around on the rocks near the shore. The Seal Rocks are three in number, of considerable size and very high, a few hundred feet from the shore, and which have been taken possession of by a colony of seals and sea-lions, which congregate here in thousands. They are quite fearless, play many antics on the rocks and in the water, bark, and amuse the people very much. If they should happen to be disturbed they take to the water very quickly by rolling and tumbling over each other in a most awkward and ludicrous manner until the water is reached. If the way of escape is cut off and they are interfered with, we were told that they become very fierce and use their sharp teeth in a very dangerous way. They are not of the Alaska variety, but become very large, reaching twelve feet sometimes. These animals are protected by law from molestation so that the colony and amusement are likely to be perpetual unless there should be a foreign invasion. We sometimes see specimens of these creatures in the menageries and Zoo Gardens in the east.

The view of the setting sun from this point is supremely grand. The vessels of all kinds and sizes are seen almost constantly going in and coming out of the Golden Gate because of the vast amount of commerce between the countries of Asia, the islands of the Pacific, the west coast of America, and San Francisco. The Pacific Ocean, so called from its placid waters, was somewhat ruffled by a stiff breeze. A road passes from the Cliff House down to the water's edge. We descended and dipped our hands and bathed our faces in the waters of the ocean, which more than three hundred years ago was discovered and taken possession of by Vasco Nunez de Balboa in the name of the King of Spain; and since the days of Magellan's voyage it has been a field of discovery, conquest, annexation by the civilized nations of the earth, and has seen the instillation of civilization in many lands, while at the same time the natives are melting away, soon to be in oblivion. What food for the contemplative mind.

To return from the Cliff House at this season of the year is far from being easy because of the vast crowds. The passengers are crowded into a room of just the capacity of the train; the room is then closed against all others. When all is ready the people are released and enter the train, which starts off, and another train comes for its portion. This is done to insure safety and prevent over crowding, but once in the crowd to get tickets and get into the room their is no return. It is like driving cattle into a narrow ally in which they cannot turn or go back preparatory to entering the slaughter house. Probably 10,000 people were there the day we made our visit. As the whole peninsula seems to be nothing but sand hills, the winds are shifting them constantly and the little railroad has to be dug out from time to time by men in constant employ for that purpose.

The stranger in San Francisco rarely leaves without a visit to Chinatown, where the colony of 6,000 or more Chinese are to be found. It is only a short distance from the centre of business and so unlike all the rest that one might suppose himself in China. Here are to be found the Celestials of the Flowery Kingdom with their pig-tails hanging down their backs, the sign of their subjugation to the Tartars, living and doing business, dressing and occupying houses precisely as if it was a part of Canton. The architecture, however, is different, with here and there an attempt at a reproduction of their home style. Frequently persons take guides to go through this section, but recognizing the general peaceful disposition of these people wherever found in eastern cities, we felt equal to an attempt to penetrate it by ourselves. So taking a cable car we were soon landed in their midst and sauntering here and there visited their shops, markets, etc. We were as much alone as if we had been in the heart of the Chinese Empire. The shops are all very small, sometimes several different tradesmen occupying the same room, the goods often of a very tawdry kind. The signs are many, suspended from the doors and windows, of various bright colors and inscribed in the peculiar language of these people. And we are told they are full of self praise and bombast with a generous sprinkling of reference to their gods, etc., reminding one of the blatant high-cockalorum in the circus whose hand bills and posters describe the most wonderful animals and marvelous performances; or the disinterested (?) patent medicine vender who from the street corners proclaims the excellence of his goods and of his sole desire to serve his fellow man in distress.

The people carry on the various kinds of business from banker, broker, lawyer, physician, and the various mercantile and manufacturing enterprises, provision dealer, laborer, laundry, to domestic servant in any capacity among the whites, etc. Where they work for themselves it is in their native way, but where they are employed by others, they follow directions to the letter as if they were machines set to do certain work in a certain way, and it being impossible to do otherwise. The story of the sailor in China whose pantaloons having become well worn and had been patched, went to a Chinese tailor to get a new pair to be made just like the worn ones, and so faithfully did the tailor follow directions that the new garment was patched precisely like the old one, is an illustration of the above fact.

Their markets were peculiar in many ways; articles were there of which we had never seen the like before and did not know how they could be used, and our knowledge of Chinese was so limited that we did not inquire, "John, washee, washee?" not being appropriate to a knowledge of provisions. Fish and vegetables are their favorites, but we did not see strings of "rats and mice, and puppies for pies." We did not visit their Joss House or places for idols though all private houses have their own idols as well. Here Paganism is practiced in the heart of a civilized and we hope christian community. Their theatres got none of our attention, as our time was limited and besides it is not always proper for ladies; parties of gentlemen frequently go, and curious ladies sometimes.

Of the vices of these people we know nothing; even had we witnessed any we should not desire to relate them. Suffice it that John Chinaman copies somewhat from his christian (?) brother, and the christian brother adopts some of the worst of heathen John's peculiarities. Many of these people are huddled together in a manner that is almost beyond belief; from cellars to garrets, every apartment, even sub cellars and excavations under the streets are occupied by them, as bad or worse than the Aleutian Islanders or Kamschatdales. In some of the subterranean rooms, lepers, filthy and loathsome, are said to be confined from the light of day and the sight of man, and where they labor until the eyes become sightless, the hands and feet drop off or melt away under this great oriental scourge.

Desirous of procuring some memento of our visit, we entered several establishments where gold ornaments are made, and upon inquiring the price of an article a small pair of scales was immediately produced and the object weighed, then the peculiar calculating machine of these people was brought into requisition and in a few moments the price was named, from which there was no deviation. The calculating machine is a frame the size of a school-boy's slate with wires upon which are strung balls, and by sliding these balls according to the Chinese way, the calculation is made. We at last saw a ring, the workmanship of which was peculiar, having fish, crabs, scorpions, etc., in high relief, and a purchase was made by the assistance of a Chinaman present who understood a little English. We had been assured that any article of jewelry purchased from these people we could rely upon as genuine, and we saw them at work about their little furnaces, melting the material preparatory to making the article which is generally made of nearly pure gold, between 22 and 24 carats fine. While in these places small crowds of Chinese gathered about the

doors and inside, apparently viewing us as curiosities and desirous of knowing our business among them; but they were well behaved and courteous.

We left this quarter highly pleased and feeling that more time would be an advantage. Most of these Chinese came here under contract and under the auspices of several companies for mining, railroad building, etc., and that in case of death their bones and bodies are to be returned to China. Women are also imported in like manner under contract and generally for immoral purposes. This species of slavery has been in great measure checked by an act of Congress preventing the landing of any Chinaman who is to become a resident of this country. In spite of the opposition to them they have done much as laborers to make California a success, as they have generally been tractable, capable of sustaining considerable hardship, uncomplaining, requiring but little food and demanding but light wages. All these have been the causes of the prejudice against them, and those who have cried out the loudest in denouncing them have themselves been foreigners.

We made a tour of the banking and broker district of the city and saw in the windows gold coins of all nations, gold quartz and gold in dust, grains and nuggets. We never saw so much gold as was displayed in the windows, arranged in trays, saucers, bottles, etc., according to the state it is in. This has been gathered in trade by individuals in the mining regions where coin is not current and the prices of goods rated at a certain weight's worth of dust, which is weighed at the time the purchase is made. It is said that in these regions a miner going into a bar room for a drink would put down a buckskin bag of dust from which the barkeeper would weigh out his pay and return the bag less the amount. Gold gathered in this way, as well as the miner's accumulations, is carried to San Francisco and other places and sold to brokers and others. The uncoined gold whether in quartz or dust, etc., is all sold by weight according to the assay of the specimen. In a jewelry store we made a few purchases of gold quartz set in ornaments as souvenirs of the trip to the El Dorado, the land of gold, and besides the gold quartz is by no means so plenty as a few years ago and will grow more rare unless new deposits are found. Jewelry is rather profusely worn, as might be inferred when it can be obtained in all conditions to suit the fancy of the wearer.

Many of the greatest discoveries in the world have been the result of the merest accident, the value of which was not always immediately apparent to the discoverer, but the credit of observing the result of an accident or unintentional circumstance when man is benefitted either physically or mentally must be accorded, as but for his act, his generation at least might not have reaped the good results, but be postponed for a succeeding one. Some discoveries are inevitable, the time being the only consideration. The discovery of gold in California was an accident and was inevitable. In a mill race which had just had the water turned into it, yellow particles were noticed which excited enough curiosity to cause an examination. One piece was put into a kettle of soap which was over a fire, and after twenty-four hours it was taken out brighter than when put in, when a further test proved the material to be gold.

This discovery was made by James W. Marshall, January 19th, 1848, at Coloma, on the American River. Captain Sutter was the contractor for building the mill race and saw-mill for Marshall. Not with the speed of the electric current, but with a remarkable celerity did the news of this discovery become noised abroad, the world heard the story, and within a year began that wonderful invasion by people from all parts of the world to seek adventure and make a fortune, and the "Forty-niners" are as proud of their early connection with the gold excitement of that period as if they were of noble birth. The stories of successes and losses, of glee and despair, are not for us to write of; we remember the time when every one discussed the prospects and probabilities. A wayward or adventurous son was perhaps permitted to try his fortune in the hope that the severe experience would tame his restless disposition; the wicked and rough, always in the advance guard, made up a large number; gentle, carefully reared and kind-hearted were not few; men broken in fortune; such as these filled every ship, and they were not few, starting on the long journey "around the Horn," or crossing the Isthmus of Panama, destined for San Francisco and the mines. Many never returned to tell their story and many forever disappeared, their fate suspected but never discovered. In a little more than two years the population of California had so increased that it was admitted into the Union as a state, and its growth since has been one of continued prosperity and population which is marvellous.

Captain Sutter participated in the glory of this discovery and the early mining efforts, and had amassed some wealth, but he died in Pennsylvania, a very few years ago, and if our memory is correct he was in comparative poverty. Mining,

at first reckless and wasteful has been reduced to a system, discarded places and material are worked over, mountains have been washed down and valleys and meadows filled by the debris, and watercourses turned to the detriment of other property, so that state laws have been enacted to regulate it.

Coin, and particularly gold, is the currency of the realm, but green-backs now pass current. The introduction of the cent has been combatted and successfully resisted; cents are not seen except as curiosities and can only be used in the post-offices. A nickel (five cent piece) is the smallest coin used. No change is ever returned where a purchase is made of less value than five cents or the multiple of five, as a purchase amounting to thirty-seven cents would have to be paid with forty cents, this is of course to the advantage of the dealer, but as this practice is universal it equalizes itself in the community. Dimes, which are coined at our mint, we call "ten-cent pieces."

When asking the price of goods of any kind and the value is twenty-five cents, the answer will be "two-bits," and four, six and eight bits for fifty and seventy-five cents and one dollar respectively, a "bit" representing twelve and one-half cents. How this antiquated method of reckoning should be continued in this new country with so many new people from different parts of the country and world, is hard to understand. We in the east have long since discarded it, though we still remember the "levy" or "eleven-penny bit" and the "fip" or "fip penny bit" representing twelve and one-half and six and one-fourth cents respectively. The younger generation know nothing about them. Gold notes were largely used in California during the war of the Rebellion, but greenbacks received no encouragement.

To pass over the fruits would be a gross neglect. Caleb and Joshua were never in California or they would never have been able to carry their load back without the assistance of a freight train or telegraph for assistance from the home guard. California has a reputation for the finest and largest fruits, and while we did not see apples, pears, oranges, etc., as big as pumpkins, nor pumpkins so large that we have read that their insides were hollowed out and fed to the cattle, and that the shell then served for a barn to house the cattle in, yet we did see the profusion and quality of peaches, plums, apricots, figs, etc., which, except the first, are nearly all rarities with us. They were placed before us on the hotel table in every form; they were for sale on the street at most moderate prices at so much per pound (for they do not sell by measure here); we were reluctant to leave behind these luscious products. All tropical and semi-tropical fruits are raised in California. Olives, figs, dates, grapes, oranges, lemons, etc., requiring a warm temperature are cultivated here in plantations, and their reputation for quality is unrivalled.

The climate of San Francisco is generally mild, rarely getting very hot or very cold. The average temperature for the year is about 54° Farenheit. The winter is the rainy season, from November to May, and the rain is rarely excessive, generally falling at night. From May to November there is almost no rain, but every morning the atmosphere is hazy and sometimes foggy, which deposits a certain amount of moisture equal to dew. The day we went to the Cliff House the wind was strong and quite cold, men carried or wore their overcoats in the street, ladies dressed in furs and other heavy robes, while those who drove had heavy fur lap coverings and blankets. Very light summer dresses are rarely worn either by men or women. In the winter we are told that the grass is green and the flowers bloom; frost is rare and very light, while snow is almost never seen.

There are many persons living in San Francisco and vicinity who have never seen snow. We subsequently met a young man who took part of the tour with us who hoped when he got among the mountains to see some snow; he had been reared a few miles from San Francisco. The mildness of climate just mentioned does not extend all over California, but the coast is generally temperate from the trade winds and warm ocean currents which course along, but back in the mountains the winters are rigorous, and snow falls to the depth we only know of by reading, but in the southern mountains the snow melts out quickly; in the north it is not so soon removed. Our limit of time having expired we concluded to pack up and "move on" with Yosemite Valley as the objective point, so having our luggage checked to Sacramento, we left San Francisco at 3:30 p. m., crossed the bay to Oakland, to take the train for Medara on the Southern Pacific Railroad.

Oakland, so called in consequence of the clumps of oak trees found in the vicinity, constitutes a suburb of San Francisco and is the residence of many business men in the latter city. It contains car shops and other buildings appropriate to the terminus of a great railroad. There are also churches, hotels, banks, factories, etc., in such numbers, size and style, as to proclaim it a place of great enterprise and wealth, and prospectively a city of great importance in itself as well as to San Francisco, and relatively the same as Jersey City is to New York. The shipping is extensive and capable of unrestrained growth, possessing many advantages over the metropolis. Here is the longest wooden pier in the world, and including mole and trestle is three miles long, accommodating eleven railway tracks; part has been filled in with rock and earth to the distance of nearly two miles. The stranger is struck with wonder at this pier extending so far straight out into the bay. At the western end is one of the largest and finest depots we have been in, and is for the overland and other traffic. Here the ferry boats from San Francisco land, and both the depot and the boats are so constructed that the upper deck of the boats is reached directly from the second story of the former where the passenger's waiting rooms are located, passengers passing from the lower deck to the wharf, there is no confusion. A freight boat starts from the old wharf near by which can accommodate twenty loaded freight cars and twenty cattle cars at one time.

Following the eastern shore of San Francisco Bay, San Pablo Bay, Straits of Carquinez for thirty-three miles, we pass Benicia and Suisun Bay into which Sacramento and San Joaquin rivers empty, and at Antioch we turn southeasterly to Lathrop where we take supper, then retiring to our sleeping berth we continue southward in the Valley of the San Joaquin River and at 2:30 a. m. arrive at Medara, one hundred and seventy-three miles from San Francisco, where our car was detached and run on a side track. Here we remained until morning, when leaving the car we took breakfast, and at 6 a. m. left in a six horse stage with twelve passengers for Wa-Wo-Na. We were soon miles away from Medara coursing over a level barren plain and at eighteen miles the first change of horses was made; we then approach the foot hills of the Sierra Nevadas, ascend among them, winding around cliffs, approach the edges of precipices which on the narrow road, seems like courting destruction, the wheels of the stage often not having six inches to spare from the edge, yet accidents are exceedingly rare. The horses tear along at a rapid and apparently reckless rate, but we were informed that a slower pace would be more dangerous for the curves, which are many and short, would cause them to become entangled, the wheels to lock under the stage and a pitch of animal and vehicle would be almost inevitable. To ride with the driver is quite a privilege and it was accorded to me part of the way; the driver and the horses are well acquainted, the former knows what they can do and the horses know what is expected of them and when.

The driver handles the reins and wields his long whip with wonderful dexterity and precision; he even has little pebbles which, with great accuracy he throws at the forward horses striking them on the ears, etc., when they are beyond the reach of his whip, or when he merely wishes to slightly remind them of his presence. Six changes of horses were made during this day and at Wa-Wo-Na, formerly called "Clark's," we stopped for the night, having made seventy miles. The road we passed over is good for this section, but is very rough as almost all mountain roads must be, and we were high up in the Sierras. It was not always possible to keep our seats or prevent our heads from striking the top of the stage when a wheel struck a stone pretty vigorously; indeed it is a little trying on thin and bald-headed persons, and we would recommend anyone contemplating this trip to make appropriate provisions for the occasion, should he be deficient in head covering and *adipose*. In addition to the roughness of the road, in this dry season the dust rises in clouds enveloping the stage and everything in it. We made an endeavor at each opportunity to get out of the stage and wash off this accumulation which makes every person the same color as his neighbor. Faces and clothes were of the same shade. We were told to dust ourselves off on the same principle as the residents of Pittsburg and similar sooty places, blow off the specs of smut which are continually rained through the atmosphere, as to otherwise interfere with them would be to become more soiled and streaked. We, however, took our chances and washed to get the worst off as well as to be refreshed.

At the dinner station where the horses are also changed we met the stage coming from Wa-Wo-Na; at the change stations there is little else than the few necessary buildings or shanties for the accommodation of horses, attendants, etc.; the horses are ready harnessed when the stage comes up, so that they can be immediately hitched to the stage when the others are detached, and so little time is lost; watering stations are placed at appropriate distances and are forlorn in their loneliness, for excepting the stages few vehicles or persons use this road. At the change stations the male passengers frequently get out to get the kinks out of their legs, but were generally in their places when "All ready" was called, save one, a young gentleman before mentioned as never having seen snow; he would start off on

a brisk trot and so continue in advance of the stage for a couple of miles, cutting off curves when informed such was possible, and when tired would be taken aboard. As we got up higher in the mountains the precipices beside the road became more appalling, and the trees became larger and larger; as we advanced pines from three to eight feet in diameter and with stems perfectly straight and rising to a height of between one hundred and two hundred feet, redwoods and other varieties in great numbers, and we measured the precipices by the number of tree lengths as they stood on the mountain side below us.

At Wa-Wo-Na is a large hotel of frame, very commodious and first class for here; there is a large plat of ground in front, which being irrigated has a delightful bed of grass a pleasant relief after a dry and dusty journey; an art gallery with some fine oil paintings furnishes an attraction to the place, also a saw-mill; these constitute the settlement. After shaking off the dust we washed, took supper, and then to bed to rest our bodies, our eyes and our brains. The next morning we again set out, now on a down grade, winding in and out on the mountain sides, passing over narrow ledges, near frightful declivities, many hundreds of feet down, making one feel uncomfortable to look over and think that barely more than the width of the tire of the wheel separates him from an almost certain death should the wheel slip over. Still the horses tear along. At some points the ledge is so narrow that by means of heavy timbers and rock the road is extended to a sufficient width. So we proceed until we arrive at Inspiration Point some eight miles from the valley and three thousand feet above it.

Inspiration Point is practically at the entrance of Yosemite Valley and high up on its edge with mountains still higher on one side of the road while on the other is a precipice nearly three-fourths of a mile down which is enough to inspire awe, and if bold enough to approach its edge you return quickly with a shudder; however this is not the inspiration, but at this high point we get a first view of the Yosemite which bursts suddenly upon the gazer. To see this picture of loveliness, wonder and grandeur inspires one with reverence at the majesty of the Creator who willed this to be so; and profound silence or an exclamation of "Oh! Oh!" is probably the only disturbance of that rapture which impresses and inspires the stranger. The stage stopped some minutes and gave us a good view from this place. Immediately before you, but in the distance you see Bridal Veil

Fall, Yosemite Fall, Cataract Fall, Cloud's Rest and Cathedral Spires. We then started down what is little more than a a steep trail, the horses going at a rattling pace and at each turn we saw more and more of the valley as we descend into the basin, until at 12:30 p. m. we were landed at Cook's Hotel in the valley and immediately in front of the Yosemite Fall. Upon landing we were immediately attacked by sundry attaches who captured our luggage and then came at us with brooms to remove the dirt we had gathered up, before we went into the house. After a wash we took dinner and then went out to see the glories of this wonderful place.

The Yosemite Valley is a huge cleft in the Sierra Nevada mountains and runs transversely across the range; it is about seven miles long and from one-half to one and a half miles wide; its bottom is about four thousand feet above sea level and is walled in by mountains of bare and solid rock ranging from one thousand to five thousand feet high; the Merced River flows throughout it, while trees, grass and flowers extend from side to side. The characteristic features of this valley are the great height of the almost perpendicular walls, the number and great height of the waterfalls, the small amount of debris or broken rock scattered throughout, making it quite easy for visitors to go around on foot. The walls have various prominent parts projecting above the rest, and according to certain forms and positions they have received names to designate them. These names are Indian, Spanish and English, the former being according to the peculiarities and traditions of that people which we need not mention here; the same applies to the names of the waterfalls.

El Capitan, the great chief or captain of the valley, is a projecting mass of solid rock 2,973 feet high; this rock it is said, can be seen from the San Joaquin Valley; it stands to the left of the entrance by the Mariposa trail. Next but at some distance from El Capitan is the Cathedral Rock, 2,660 feet high, surmounted by two pinnacles of rock extending 800 feet higher. Next follow the Three Brothers, a mass of rock with three slightly inclined peaks the tallest of which is 3,830 feet above the valley. Next we have the Sentinel Rock shaped somewhat like an obelisk, rising 3,270 feet. Farther on we find the North Dome, the name suggesting somewhat its shape, rising 3,568 feet above the valley. The South Dome still more majestic rises to 4,737 feet above the valley and has one vertical face of over 1500 feet from the summit, while the lower part is nearly so.

The Cap of Liberty is 4,600 feet high, and Star King 5,600 feet. About a mile east of South Dome is Glacier Point 3,700 feet above the valley, with Cloud's Rest on the south wall, rising to 6,450 feet, the highest point here and 10,500 feet above sea level. We approached the bases of a few of these wonderful masses of granite and were impressed with wonder and admiration; they are too great for the mind to appreciate their immensity in a short time; time only could develop that particular feeling, for they grow with each hour spent in their presence. Those which we did not go directly to were distinctly visible from one point or another in the valley where we did go.

There are trails reaching to Cloud's Rest, Glacier Point and other places, and horses and guides are obtainable for that purpose, but to ride around the mountain sides on the most dangerous and narrowest of trails and at heights, where when viewed from the bottom of the valley, the horses and riders appear little larger than flies, did not seem a strong enough inducement, for none but the clear-headed and brave-hearted we were assured would dare to undertake the trip; but the views to be obtained from these elevated points are wonderfully grand and sublime, and unequaled so far as known; we were told our visit would not be complete without undertaking it. The whole valley lies at your feet and beyond are the rocky Sierras. Think of being on a trail of three feet wide or less (and three feet is regarded as a good width) on a rock shelf 1000 feet or more above the valley, where the rock is almost perpendicular, and where a horse cannot turn around or the rider dismount, where, whatever the number, none could render assistance, as for instance if you got dizzy or had a faint, and there will be no surprise that we did not venture, though our determination was arrived at with reluctance. Many places are absolutely inaccessible, at least they have not yet been reached, but some of the domes, rocks and spires are visited, but their tops cannot be scaled without imperiling life, for the summits are naught but bare, unbroken rock which lichen could hardly hold fast upon and a fly had better rest content with a bald head than attempt to settle upon one of these. The South Dome has been scaled and some enterprising individual (I might say fool-hardy as well) has anchored at various points 975 feet of rope to enable any ambitious person to hold on to and accomplish the daring feat. Were there elegant stairs and strong hand rail it would be no trifling matter to climb so high. A woman has been one of the few who have reached the top of South Dome.

The falls are scarcely less awe inspiring than the rocks. Bridal Veil has a clear fall of 630 feet, striking upon a mass of rocks from which it is again precipitated 300 feet perpendicular making 930 feet from the top. This is one of the most beautiful in the valley, and as the water descends its edges swayed and broken by the winds resemble the serpent rockets which we formerly saw on 4th of July evenings; the unbroken body sways gently like a thin tissue moved by wind.

The Yosemite Fall is also divided, but in three parts instead of two as in the Bridal Veil; the first part is a clear fall of nearly 1600 feet, striking a ledge of rock, over which it flows in a series of small cascades for 626 feet more, and then 400 feet in perpendicular to the bottom. This is said to be the highest waterfall in the world for an equal body of water; the water where it comes over the top is estimated at twenty feet wide, two feet deep and falling at the rate of 500,000 cubic feet an hour. This body of water which starts almost thread-like in appearance as it comes more into view, has the peculiar swaying that is so beautiful in the Bridal Veil, and as these two falls are the only ones in the valley possessing this feature, it is probably due to the perpendicular fall or their situation in relation to prevailing winds. The mind may picture but the eye must see to appreciate these beautiful falls. No description ever can convey the complete idea. Vernal Fall is a beautiful *little* fall of 350 feet (when we speak so familiarly of thousands of feet, 350 feet become almost contemptible.) Niagara Falls are only about 160 feet high, but the volume of water is infinitely greater. Nevada Fall, over 600 feet, is veritably grand. Other falls are seen here and there, but they are as threads. The falls are supplied by the melting snows in the mountains beyond, and during the months of May and June are seen to their best advantage. As September comes on the water decreases, the falls become lessened in volume and a few of the smaller ones dry up. Their water makes up the body of the Merced River which runs through the valley.

An episode connected with our visit I will here relate. We were wandering about in search of whatever might interest, when we came upon a little cabin sheltered by trees, vines, etc., and seeing no one about we made bold to trespass, but not to enter the house. A pair of antlers hung outside and we thought what a nice souvenir of the occasion they would be if we could obtain them; while pondering upon the probability of becoming their possessor the door of the cabin opened and there to our surprise stood not a grizzly bear nor a wild Indian, but a kindly faced man, about sixty-five years of age, dressed as a gentleman would be in any city and about to take a walk. His kindly voice reassured us and we expressed our desire to purchase the antlers. "Money," he said "could not buy them, they should be ours for the taking." We protested, but he was equally firm, consenting at last to receive a book if we thought enough of it to send him one. We were introduced into his cabin, saw many evidences of refinement and education and learned that this was Mr. T. M. Hutchings the superintendent of the valley. Here in the valley he remains year in and year out, cut off from all the world in winter except by telephone, and in the summer by the incoming of tourists and the United States mail. His history is one of much sadness; he is alone and he seems to love to be alone to commune with himself, with nature and with God. A pleasant interchange of letters has since been had with him which makes us wish we knew him more intimately, he is highly educated, carries on an extensive correspondence with all parts of the world. We saw in his hand a bundle of over forty letters which he was about to deposit in the mail bag, they being answers to inquiries respecting the Yosemite Valley. He loves to be busy not merely for the pleasure of occupation, but to divert his mind from those heart clouds which oppress him.

When the winter snows fill the roadways, trails, and even the valley sometimes to a depth of fifteen or twenty feet he employs his leisure time in making snow shoes for man and horse. The snow shoes for man are made of three-fourth inch pieces of wood, from five to six feet long and six inches wide, turned up in front and provided with straps to hold the feet. Then with a pole the wearer slides over the snow, the pole serving to propel or retard according as to whether he goes up or down an incline, also to steady him on the level. Snow shoes for horses will strike one as very comical if not absurd, but we saw some he had made. The shoe consists of a block of wood about fifteen inches square and two inches thick, with a shoe fitted in the top and so arranged as to clasp the horse's hoof; the animal soon learns to use these awkward contrivances so that they may not fall. Snow shoes are required because early in the spring season it becomes necessary to open the roads, clear away the snow and even tunnelling when otherwise too deep, so that entrance to the valley can be made from the outside world, besides the sooner the road is opened the sooner the visitors enter, hence the greater profit, and too as the country along the road from Medara is as yet but slightly productive, all the provisions used along the road and in the valley must be carried in. Only a few persons remain in the valley during the winter, hence is very lonely except to the seeker after solitude.

The Yosemite Valley was first entered by white men in 1848 and afterwards in 1850 and 1852 Mr. Hutchings was the second white man who entered it, and if we are correctly informed, he has been a resident ever since. He had a small hotel for the accommodation of the few visitors in its early days when it was more of a venture than now. It was several years after its discovery before its wonders were published to the world since which time it has grown in popularity, and by those who have seen many natural wonders in all parts of the world it is said that the Yosemite Valley stands alone and unrivalled of its kind. There were some English tourists in our party in the coach, who had just come from India and China and their expressions were most enthusiastic.

The Valley is now an established part of the State and is governed by Commissioners appointed by state authority; this will preserve it forever from vandalism though not much could be done towards demolishing or damaging its granite walls, yet some enterprising advertising agent might venture to paint the name and virtues of some wonderful remedy as "Mexican Mustang Liniment" particularly useful for those who visiting the valley, desire instantaneous relief from bruises received in the stage or from tumbles on the rocks; or of some wonderful soap compound particularly useful for travellers to remove the dust and dirt after the return from the Valley; or that "John Wanamaker s largest retail store in America, can supply all the necessary wants in his line for such a journey and have plenty left to replace all things torn, worn out, or lost, on the return," upon the dome of El Capitan or other almost inaccessible point, for visitors to view with their glasses.

Mirror Lake is a small but beautiful sheet of water, in which, when the water is still, can be seen the reflection of the surrounding trees and mountains; there is nothing remarkable in this, the same is often seen in stil streams and lakes elsewhere. With our antlers (which came from a deer shot in the valley), a couple of sticks for canes and a few other trifles, we climbed into the stage and going back the way we came, stopped at Inspiration Point, turned to take a last look at the wonderful, beautiful, and flowery Yosemite Valley which we may never see again. I neglected to say that wild flowers of great beauty and variety exist in profusion and the floral botanist would be in his glory to spend a month here among them. An attempt to press a few proved a failure, for we were not provided with materials for that purpose. At noon time we arrived at Wa-Wo-Na and after dinner we again took the stage and a nine mile drive brought us to the famous Mariposa Grove of Big Trees.

The road from Medara to the Yosemite Valley passes among trees which in the mountains attain enormous proportions, pines and cedars particularly, the former ranging from three to twenty feet in diameter. It is no wonder then that at first we were not so much impressed with the bigness of the Big Redwoods, besides they stand among trees of immense size. But by standing beside them walking about them, going into and through them we gradually felt how much greater these were than any we had ever seen. Did they stand alone in some open field their magnitude would be displayed to better advantage; perhaps the surrounding trees have been the means of preserving these mammoth specimens from destruction by the violent storms which prevail in these high altitudes at certain seasons. Forest fires do much toward destroying the young ones in other parts. Many of these monarchs of the forest are much injured by fire at their bases which is regarded as remarkable, for there are no evidences of having attacked other trees adjacent and it is said that probably these fires occurred hundreds of years ago. One of the trees has a roadway cut through its base, and under it we passed in our six horse coach, as it is on the line of the road into the grove. Whether the road was built purposely to thus go through it or whether it acted as an obstruction and was tunnelled in consequence, we cannot say. One fallen tree has a stairway leading to the upper side which has a platform built upon it. Almost all the fallen trees are more or ess broken because the wood is quite brittle, in the few instances where they are not broken it is supposed they fell when there was much snow in the mountain. A tree in the Calaveras Grove has been felled in order to determine if possible its age, and required the labor of five men for twenty-two days using long augurs to penetrate towards the heart; thus weakened it still stood so plumb that even wedging was required to topple it over. It is computed that one of the Big Trees would yield over 500,000 feet of one inch sawed lumber. A section of one of the Big Trees from the Fresno Group was exhibited at the Centennial Exposition, and it is to be regretted that it was not purchased for the Fairmount Park. There is also another section at the New Orleans Exposition and is pictured in *Harper's Weekly.*

The trees of the Calaveras and Mariposa Groups are numbered and many are named. In the latter group we saw the Grizzly Giant. Grant, Garfield, Three Sisters, Three Brothers, Wa-Wo Na, etc. This last has the roadway cut through it. The stage stopped under it and we procured (what an old salt would call) a "splinter" from it by the use of an axe. Much as we are opposed to violation of the law, and depreciate vandalism, yet our American relic-hunting disposition could not be quelled.

The largest of these trees measure from 50 to 91.6 feet in circumference at their bases, but two of the largest have been so much burned that their original measure of over 100 feet is very much lessened; one of these, the Grizzly Giant, we measured with a string as high as we could reach above the ground and it was 82 feet. The highest Big Tree is in the Calaveras Group, 325 feet high; the highest in the Mariposa Group is 272 feet and the Grizzly Giant is the oldest thus far found in any group. These trees are perfectly straight and devoid of branches until about one hundred feet from the ground and we saw branches said to be six feet in diameter which we verified by comparing them with the fallen trees. Further destruction of this grove will be prevented so far as man is concerned as the United States made a grant of two square miles containing this group to the State of California as trustee, for a public park.

The Big Trees are only found in the Sierra Nevadas in California and at an average elevation of between 4,000 and 5,000 feet above the sea, in groups in a belt of about 200 miles; whether known to white men before the cession of this country to the United States, we do not know, but it was not until about 1850 that the world was apprised of their existence.

The Big Trees are known to botanists as the *Sequoia Gigantea*, named after Sequo-yah a half breed Cherokee Indian who was born in the last century, and was a man of remarkable intelligence, but we did not learn that he had anything to do with the discovery or description of the giants. The *Sequoia Sempervirens* is a very near relation of the *Gigantea* and is generally in its company, though it has a most extensive range, covering hundreds of miles of mountain and very numerous. They belong to the Conifera or cone bearing trees, and resemble the cypress; the wood is red like

cedar and is hence called the Redwood, light in weight, rather brittle, and resists decay with astonishing power. The bark is of a reddish brown color, quite porous and somewhat fibrous, is from twelve to twenty inches thick, the cones are small (from one and three-fourth to two and a half inches long) growing in large numbers in clusters; they are hard and compact, containing many seeds which are strikingly small when compared with the size of the tree, one-fourth inch long and one-sixteenth inch wide and as thin as paper.

While the *Sequoia Gigantea* exists in large numbers in the various groves the giants are but a comparatively speaking, small part. There are many in their "youthful vigor" of ten feet in diameter, supposed to be about 500 years old. 'Tis like children among their grandsires. The ages of the largest trees are estimated at between 1200 and 2000; what an age for a living thing! Nations have died, races become extinct, discoveries made, revolutions religious and civil, civilization advancing, requiring centuries, and yet these survive and with reasonable prospect of centuries yet going over their crowns, before they pass the way of all living things. Other trees of great size exist among these great ones, as sugar pines, spruce, fir, bastard cedar (which is very like the Sequoia) and others. The most of these become very large, the sugar pines, (*pinus lambertini*,) growing to 250 feet or more in height and from 10 to 20 feet in diameter, the cones of which are 12 to 20 inches in length and from 4 to six inches in diameter. We gathered up several, sixteen inches long. They resemble the common pine cone of the east except their great size; they are supposed by many to come from the giant trees. This may arise from the fact that they are found in those groves and also that it would be a demonstration of the seeming fitness of things. These pines, etc., are fitting associates of scarcely more attractive giants.

We purchased at a little cabin in the grove (there being no other houses) two of the large cones encased in strips of redwood, as souvenirs. These with other cones, large and small, gathered from the ground we finished our visit, and with our company left in the stage for Wa-Wo-Na, took supper and the next morning commenced our all day ride to Medara. A peculiar tree of small size, generally little more than a shrub with a leaf something like the mountain laurel, found in the Yosemite Valley. In the mountains and along the roadside is the Manzanita, remarkable for its crookedness, little more than a foot of straight wood in any part. It is of exceeding toughness and hardines, being almost of the density of box-wood. It almost resists the saw and axe. We procured with great difficulty a few pieces; an endeavor to procure a straight piece for a cane proved fruitles, and an offer to the stage driver of a fee if he would cut a stick for us was declined; securing an ax, we tried for ourselves and while fairly successful in getting some pieces it was, however, with great difficulty. When the trunks are moderately thick, canes are sometimes sawed from them, but neccessarily having a cross grain in some part, they readily break. We saw such a demonstration in the hands of one of our company. The manzannita grows in bunches as if a number came from a common root, and rarely reach ten feet high. It produces a berry, said to be eatable, but we did not try; the bark is of a dark red color, which, when the tree is cut at this season, peels off in thin scales, revealing a green underlayer which also peels; when it is cut in winter the bark adheres very closely and makes the wood very attractive.

The journey to Medara was made without special incident except to hear the expressions of surprise and satisfaction made by several of our party who were subjects of John Bull. They had traveled much and England was great, but they had nothing at home, nor had they seen abroad anything which would compare with what they had just left. The Big Trees may have been alive, though very young when Julius Cæsar invaded Britain, and were centuries old when William the Conqueror first set foot on British soil. These remarks were very pleasant to our American ears.

On the return from as well as on the way to the Valley we passed under and near to a large flume which extends from Medara up into the mountains a distance of seventy miles; for a considerable number of miles it follows the stage road very closely. This flume is built like a trough in a pig-sty and is about six feet across the top; in some places it is nearly on a level with the road and at others where it crosses gullies it is supported on trestles nearly one hundred feet high. It is used to carry lumber from the saw mills in the mountains down to Medara. It has sundry stations along its course where it widens somewhat and where persons are stationed with telegraphic and telephonic instruments, so as to observe and announce accidents or other circumstances when they occur, just after the manner of a signal station on a railway line. The water, besides being used for running lumber is also used for irrigation by persons who purchase the right

from the flume owners. The water runs with great swiftness as might be supposed where the grade is so great and the conductor so smooth, as it must be to prevent jamming of lumber. Occasionally trips are taken from the mountains in triangular-shaped boats made for the purpose, but this amusement is not only dangerous, but a wetting is an almost sure result, while the transit is of almost lightning-like rapidity. A trip had been made down this flume a day or two before we got there. A comical adventure was related some time ago in the New York *Tribune* by H. J. Ramsdell, who in company with Messrs. Flood and Fair, the California millionaires, and others, had been visiting the mines near Virginia City, Nevada, and a flume ride was proposed and accepted. He says: "I thought that if men worth $25,000,000 or $30,000,000 a piece could afford to risk their lives I could afford to risk mine, which was not worth half as much." The average time made was thirty miles an hour, and after a fifteen mile ride in thirty-five minutes, he, like the rest, was all wet, and the other impression that they received can be better appreciated by the following: "Flood said he would not make the trip again for the whole Consolidated Virginia Mine."

This day's ride was made in a temperature greater than we ever experienced and when we arrived at Medara in the evening we were informed that the thermometer had registered 118 degrees Fahrenheit. After supper, with our horns, canes, sticks, etc., we got into a sleeping car in waiting and retired to dream of great rocks and huge trees but we had no night-mares; later in the night the train from Southern California hooked us on and away we sped up the San Joaquin Valley to Lathrop. As daylight appeared our eyes opened on a country which was under cultivation, wheat being the principal production, there being fields of it for miles and still standing; few houses were to be seen anywhere and they are the merest shanties. The grass, which is green in the winter and spring becomes naturally cured in the summer and is cut for hay; the rainfall is light and where it fails irrigation is resorted to, artesian wells and streams supplied with windpumps furnishing the water. Trees are few except on the mountain slopes. The San Joaquin Valley lies between the Sierra Nevada and the coast ranges of mountains, with a width of from twenty to one hundred and fifty miles, and extends from Lathrop southward two hundred and fifty miles. The soil is a close loam which, under the summer sun, opens in great cracks and of considerable depth. The stations along the road are all small, being side tracks, telegraph stations and occasionally villages.

We arrive at Lathrop at 7 a. m., take our breakfast and change cars for Sacramento, which we reached at 10:30 a. m. August 11th. Lathrop is a railroad town of great importance, it being on one of the routes from Sacramento to San Francisco, also being at the entrance of the San Joaquin Valley, traversed by the Southern Pacific Railroad, by which the Yosemite and Southern California is reached.

Stockton, a short distance above Lathrop, is on very low level ground and is an active business place; the railroad passes to the east of it, a deep slough navigable for large steamers and other vessels connecting with the San Joaquin river, enables it to carry on considerable shipping trade with San Francisco. The country hereabouts is mostly under cultivation, wheat being the staple product, though other things, as vegetables, are raised, but no corn. We do not remember having had green corn at any of the hotels west of Ogden. Irrigation is entirely depended on and wind-pumps are so numerous in this section of California that at one railway station (Lodi) near here we counted nearly two hundred in the few minutes of the stop of the train and it would be safe to say there are thousands in its vicinity. Stockton gets its water from an artesian well.

Sacramento, which we passed in the night on our way to San Francisco, is located on the Sacramento river, ninety miles from San Francisco, and is the capital of the state. It is elegantly laid out, the streets are broad and regular, shaded by magnificent shade trees, making in many places almost an arcade. The business houses are mostly of brick, while the residences from cottages to mansions are of wood, the redwood, the *sequoia sempervirens* being used, and we felt it a pity that these magnificent forest trees should be used for such purpose, notwithstanding their profusion. The gardens and lawns are well kept and we saw oranges, figs, limes and tropical plants growing in rare profusion. The city is lighted with gas and electricity; water works which take the water from the Sacramento river, churches, college halls, schools, courthouse, capitol and other buildings constitute the principal public edifices; the capitol, built of granite and brick, is very extensive and cost $2,500,000. The architecture resembles somewhat the capitol at Washington and is surmounted by the Temple of Liberty and a bronze statue representing California; the interior is finished in elegant

style and the Californians are justly proud of the whole. It is built in the centre of a block of ground upon an elevation which is terraced, the whole surrounded by an ornamental railing; the grounds are ornamented with shade trees and flowers and are very carefully kept. The car shops of the Central Pacific Railroad are located here, for Sacramento is the beginning of the road. Flour mills, carriage, wagon and furniture factories are numerous, but this city is probably best known for its manufacture of the famous California Blankets, those lovely, thick, soft and wooly covers which are luxurious and unlike any others manufactured in the world that we are familiar with in the east. The wool crop of California is one of the largest, finest and best in the world.

Sacramento is also famous for its packing and shipment of California fruits. We made a visit to one of the largest packing establishments in the city and there found a large number of Chinamen employed in sorting fruit, wrapping each specimen in paper, as oranges and lemons are wrapped which come to us from the south. These are carefully packed in small boxes for shipment. An inquiry was made as to why Chinamen were employed and the answer was that they followed directions and samples more closely than whites and made no deviation, which insured uniformity of size and quality of each package. They handle the fruit with the dexterity of an expert handling and packing eggs.

The hotels are numerous and very large the size of the city. Our stay at the "Western" was exceedingly satisfactory as to accommodations, table and cost. The sidewalks are all plank, and a peculiarity of the buildings near the street is that they have porticos extending from the second story out to the curb line, thus making a cover over the pavement, and as they are quite continuous they protect the pedestrian when the summer's sun is at meridian, for it sometimes gets very hot in this place; also from the showers in the rainy season.

Every town of any size on the Pacific Coast has its Chinese quarter, and Sacramento is no exception, where large numbers of these people live, transact business, or work in various parts of the city for other people. They are large dealers in fruits and vegetables, which they sell by weight and not by peck or bushel. This is universal throughout the west and not peculiar to Chinamen. They are packers, as before noted, and also act as laundrymen, cooks and chamber—shall I say maids or men? in public and private houses, in which capacities they are said to be very reliable.

Agricultural Park, with its race course, is to be seen from the road when approaching the city from the east, and it is held in high esteem here in the fair and racing season. The State Exposition Building is a large fine structure and is permanent.

The ground upon which Sacramento stands, as well as surrounding it, is very low and marshy, but its "moors and fens" which are filled with festering malaria have been so changed by filling in, draining, etc., that the place has been made habitable and the work of reclaiming is still going on, to the great advantage of the business and other interests of the city. He who has been long absent from the city would not recognize many places on his return. In the early days of the city the streets during certain seasons, from rain, overflow and retained moisture, would become so miry as to constitute a dangerous slough or sink for all who ventured, whether man or beast, and we have seen it stated that on one occasion a humane man posted a sign near one particularly bad place, which bore this significant legend :

"This street is impassable
Not even jackassable."

This man, if dead, should have a monument erected to his memory for this good deed by Mr. Henry Bergh's Society for the Prevention of Cruelty to Animals from the proceeds of the legacies his society has received ; for anything but purely selfish demonstrations was rare in the early days of California.

The shipping is quite extensive, as the Sacramento river is navigable for large vessels. Much fruit is grown in the Sacramento, Napa, and other adjacent valleys, the vineyards and orchards are extensive and it is said the wine interests alone promise to make California one of the richest states in the Union. The wine is pure, cheap and plentiful ; the choicest grapes, which in the east fetch from 50 cents to $1 per pound, are here sold for 10 cents. The more decidedly tropical fruits are raised in Southern California. Thus California outrivals any other state in the possibilities of its its culture and it is prophesied that its gold interests will eclipse the past productions of that precious metal.

The railroad depot is large and most complete. It is only excelled by that at Oakland, which is the finest on the Pacific coast. Two days spent in Sacramento gave us a fair idea of the city and we turned our faces homeward to leave this wonderland behind.

California is a state which includes all kinds of weather and season within its boundaries. The southern part is hot, with little or no rain in its desert country, and winter is unknown ; farther up towards the middle there is rain at certain seasons, but in no great quantity, and the land is fairly tillable by irrigation ; spring and summer are perpetual and the mountains may be covered with snow ; further north there is the rainy season which corresponds with our winter; the atmosphere at this season is chilly, snow is exceedingly rare and plants are always green ; still farther north the coast line is moderately warm, while in the mountains the winters are rigorous; the sheltered valleys are, however, habitable and very productive.

We did not get into the extreme north or south. California is too big and has too much of interest to be seen in a short stay like ours ; even our ride of nearly 700 miles through it showed us but a small part. We hope this may not be our last visit and if so fortunate we shall visit the great vinyards, orchards and groves to the north and the south, compared with which, what we did see is quite insignificant.

Getting into a sleeper, by the light of a waning moon we saw a little of the country east of Sacramento, but retiring we awoke next morning at 5 o'clock at Truckee, 119 miles from Sacramento. Truckee 209 miles from San Francisco is a railroad division station, having a large round-house and some repair shops. It also has a large lumber trade ; the population, about 2000, has a large number of Chinamen. It is also a mountain resort in summer time and is the point from which stages start to visit several beautiful lakes a few miles away. The hunting and fishing make the locality very attractive. In winter the snow storms are sometimes of enormous proportions and the need of snow sheds in these mountains becomes very evident, forty to fifty feet of snow sometimes covering them.

We soon passed the Nevada line and at Reno we took breakfast ; continuing over the line we came, we crossed into Utah at 1:45 a. m., Aug. 15, and at 7:30 a. m. took breakfast at Ogden. Nevada is a state erected a few years ago out of the territory of Utah, by cutting it through in the middle from north to south; the eastern half still remains as Utah Territory.

Nevada is composed of mountains and valleys, furnishing grazing ground for cattle and sheep ; forests of timber more or less stunted for want of water ; sagebrush, alkali and sandy deserts which absorbs all the water which comes from the mountains. Some few lakes exist ; but as a mining state it stands almost unrivalled, gold, silver, lead, iron, sulphur, antimony, coal and salt existing in vast quantities, and the output has been enormous; mining is still in its infancy. Carson and Virginia Cities are the great mining points of this state, The great Consolidated Virginia Mine and the Sutro Tunnel are near the latter place.

From Ogden we proceeded eastward through the wonderful Echo and Weber Canons which we were again enabled to see, not more effectively, however, than when we came out, for by the courtesy of the conductor on that occasion we saw much that would have otherwise passed without our notice. He called our attention to them as we came to them, took us to the most advantageous parts of the train for observation, sometimes on the platforms, where we could get the advantage of a view of the great heights in the narrow passes, etc. We have not got his name or we should here mention it with our thanks. Train men on the western roads are generally courteous so far as our observation goes, and it is a great comfort to find it so. The remainder of the road to Cheyenne was passed in daylight and the interesting points have already been noted. Having crossed Utah and Wyoming with their hills, desert and sage brush, at Pine Bluffs, 473 miles from Omaha, we pass into Nebraska, which presents nothing materially different in the landscape until we reach the Platte River, where we see horses, cattle and sheep in vast herds, for the Platte Valley is well provided with grass, and ranches exist on all sides. No buildings are to be seen except at the railway stations and such others as are necessary for the herders of stock.

On the way we pass through Sidney, 412 miles from Omaha. It has a round house and small repair shops, and a population of about 1,000. The next place of importance is North Platte, 291 miles from Omaha, and is said to be a thriving town of 2000 inhabitants. The largest round house and repair shops on the road are at this place; it is also noted for being the residence of Hon. Wm F. Cody (Buffalo Bill). His house was pointed out to us. North Platte is also a great centre for the shipment of cattle from the ranches in Nebraska; also for those driven up from Texas. Here we took supper and soon after retired.

On waking in the morning we found we had passed through a rain storm, which had been pretty severe, though it did not disturb us. The railroad follows the South Platte River to near North Platte, where it continues along the Platte to within a few miles of Omaha. We had crossed the Nebraska

plains famous for their buffalo herds in past days; also antelope, coyotes, prairie chickens, prairie dogs and Indians; the first have long since passed away and their place taken by horses, cattle and sheep; the other above mentioned creatures are fast melting away before the advance of white men. We saw small fleets of "prairie schooners" with their ox or mule teams slowly wending their way across these wide, wide plains. We saw roads here and there, but where they led we could only imagine, for no habitation could be seen in any direction, and here a clear uninterrupted view is had in all directions for very many miles.

The traveller, emigrant or otherwise, who is overtaken by wind, rain, hail or snow storms has no means of shelter, but must take them as they come, and it is said that they are often sudden and of a severity which we in the east can scarcely conceive possible. We also saw numerous buttes, mounds, castle and chimney rocks in various parts of the prairie. It would make one wonder what could induce anyone to venture in these apparently desolate regions, but the over crowding of the east, the necessity for food, and the desire for gain have doubtless been the real incentives as they must be in the peopling of any new country. Thus far we have not seen many people and there are many thousands of square miles of uncultivated lands, but as population increases all this will be changed

We arrived at Council Bluffs 7:55 a. m. August 17th, and put up at the Railroad Hotel connected with the depot. After a preliminary wash up and breakfast we took a horse car and went up into the town, for the town is located some distance from the station. The horse made a splash with each step he took over the ties, for the road between the tracks is not paved but has deep holes in which the rain of the previous night had accumulated, and the horse displayed considerable dexterity in avoiding the ties.

Council Bluffs, so called because of its having been the scene of a number of Indian councils, having such a great name in the east, figuring on all the railroad maps and time tables as a place of some note, attracted our attention, but we were surprised to see a comparatively small town, though it claims about 20,-000 inhabitants, with its wooden houses, many not painted, set upon stilts to keep them out of the floods which overflow the lower part of this place when it rains. The board walks are also elevated and passage ways are made to the houses. We saw many houses with water all around and under them; also signs announcing lots for sale which were then covered with water. Its prominence depends upon its being a railroad point. It is the terminus of several Iowa railroads; there is also here a large stock yard.

Getting off the car where it stopped, it turned on a turn table and went back to the depot. We took a short walk on the plank side walks and awaited the return of the car we came in, which took about one hour, for there is only one car on this line and so far as we know it is the only line. A goodly number of private residences are located on the bluff, but we found the place so generally unattractive, the streets very deep with mud and altogether not worth the trip of two miles, the distance from the depot, that we returned as soon as possible.

We then desired to go to Omaha to get our mail if any, and looked about for the ferry to cross the river but found none. We were told that the banks of the river being so low and of such soft earth that no roadway or landing place could readily be made, but that trains at stated times crossed the bridge for the accommodation of passengers and teams, flat cars being provided for the latter. Thus we crossed and going to the post office found what we were after and then took a view of the town which we found an active business place, well built and a great railroad point. It is fifty feet higher than Council Bluffs and nearer the river. The stores of both places were open notwithstanding this was Sunday, but no business was being transacted. A resident said that Sunday business was very light and that Sunday opening would eventually regulate itself.

Council Bluffs is the legal eastern terminus of the Union Pacific Railroad, but Omaha is the business point. The depot at the former place is very extensive and accommodates all the roads centering here. The railroad company owns 1000 acres, which is designed for extending the facilities and meeting the growing demands of this place. The depot hotel is large, elegant and convenient, and we recommend it to visitors to Council Bluffs.

The bridge across the Missouri at this place is an iron tru s and is an engineering marvel. It is composed of 11 spans, 250 feet each in length and 50 feet above high water mark. The spans rest on 11 piers of cast iron, 2 columns each, 8½ feet in diameter, and sunken through the mud down to bed rock, workmen being on the inside under great atmospheric pressure cleaning out the earth so as to enable the tubes to sink, one of the columns reaching the rock at 82 feet. Total length of the iron structure of the bridge is 2750 feet. The eastern approach is an embankment one and a half miles long; the western end of the bridge rests on the high bank. There must have been considerable loss of life in its construction as is the case with all large enterprises whether in building tunnels or bridges.

We had now completed 1,865 from miles San Francisco to Council Bluffs, and from our time table we found we had passed 254 stations along the line including the termini, with an aggregate population of 460,000 inhabitants. Of this amount 389,-000 belong to 7 stations (and of this last 233,000 belong to San Francisco), leaving the amount of 71,000 to be distributed among 247 stations many of which have nothing to indicate that they are stations except a sign with the name, and others—well let me quote from Robt. J. Burdette, *Hawkeye* man:

"As you wander up and down the land you observe at the stations the smaller the town the bigger the name. The poorest, most distressed, hungriest-looking passengers always get off at the smallest, forlornest towns with the biggest names. Now there is a man just got off at Canton City. He got on at Liverpool City. He didn't have enough coat to sew buttons to. His trousers were made of gunny-bags, with patches of tarpaulin and shreds of flannel, and his hat wasn't made at all. It was something that grows wild somewhere in the dark. And the city is on a par with the man. Now there is London City, that we just passed. It is a compilation of cabins and shanties, with one grocery with a dashboard in front, where the natives in the evenings hold their mouths open and say 'Hey' when any one ventures a remark relative to the price of hogs. It is the wild, ungovernable ambition of every little hamlet about the size of a piano-box, stood down in a desolate swamp or treeless flat, to choose some high-sounding name, and then tack "city" on to it. So it is that we have Boston, New York, Brooklyn and Chicago. That is all very well; but when you take a trip on the Lost Creek narrow gauge, you find Metropolis City, Berlin City, Edinburgh City, Vienna City. Not a single plain monosyllable town on the line, and not a city that can raise one hundred people to go to the circus. Still such is the way of man. I do not feel harshly toward these cities——" This is a fair description of many places we have seen. Time will make some places important while are now but barely noted on the railway maps, develop new ones, and see others blotted out.

August 18th we took the Chicago & North-Western Railroad, crossed the State of Iowa, which is a vast prairie, very fertile and with no special features. The soil is a black loam quite two feet deep, in some places more, and like much of the country in the Mississippi Valley, requires no manuring as it is of almost inexhaustible richness. We passed through several important places, particularly Cedar Rapids but as it was night and we were comfortably sleeping, we knew nothing of what was transpiring. We crossed the Mississippi River on a fine iron bridge at Clinton and continued due east across Illinois to Chicago, which we reached at 7 a. m. August 19th and 490 miles from Council Bluffs.

A few days spent in this great city in visiting Lincoln Park, taking views of Lake Michigan at various points, looking into the large dry goods houses and public buildings, all worthy the reputation which this has. This city is greater since the destructive fire some years ago. Nearly all evidence of it has been blotted out and like the phoenix rising from the ashes more glorious than ever, there have been rows of tall, fine looking and capacious buildings in the places of those destroyed. The weather became intensely hot and we concluded not to run the risk of sunstroke by pressing too much sight seeing into a short space of time, and we therefore left much unseen, for this city is very disagreeable in hot weather, located as it is on low ground which is boggy ; the hot moisture rises and is very oppressive. We however determined to visit the famous stock yards, and the slaughter and packing houses of the famous pork king Armour, who is sometimes sarcastically called the "King of the Hogs," or the "King Hog."

By cable car we were taken about two miles south west of the city and saw the immense droves of cattle and pigs in the yards. The slaughter house is a large brick building right in the midst of the yards. The slaughtering of pigs is done in the second story and is supplied with the most approved machinery for this wholesale taking of life and preparing of the meat, which, in the hands of workmen, each having his particular part to perform, acquire a dexterity which is astonishing. The pigs are raised upon an elevator to the level of the slaughtering room and each in turn is caught by the leg by a machine and hoisted into the air. A man with a long knife dexterously plunges it into the hog's throat and before he ceases his shrieks he is plunged into a trough of scalding water. While passing through it revolving wheel brushes are applied to the body and the hair is rapidly removed. Then it is hung up and quickly disembowelled. Passing on to others the head is cut off and the

body split in two. It is then washed off and starts on a railway track suspended from the ceiling to a refrigerating room. So rapidly is all this done that in the time it would take to read this account a pig has passed from his grunting selfish life to the cooing room and probably all cut up ready for packing, or shipment in the fresh state, and Armour's refrigerator cars are to be seen in all parts of the country used in the transportation of fresh dressed meats.

That this slaughter is almost beyond comprehension is best appreciated when it is said that the enormous number of between 5,000 and 6,000 are killed in a working day or nearly ten every minute. Cattle are driven into stalls from which they cannot turn, they are then shot and with a rapidity almost equal to that just described they pass from life through all the processes necessary to fit them for the market. We at first entered this establishment with some reluctance, feeling that slaughter houses are not the places which are regarded proper for ladies to visit, but our minds were soon disabused on this point, for we saw parties of ladies and gentlemen coming in carriages, or as we did, to see this place, which is probably not exceeded by any in Cincinnati or Kansas City, the other great centres of the slaughtering and packing trade.

Chicago is still growing in extent and wealth. It is the great railroad centre of the north and west ; its suburbs are decorated with magnificent private residences and ditches running here and there to drain the land. The Chicago river divides the city ; it is a narrow, deep and sluggish stream crossed by numerous draw bridges and has on each side large factories and lumber yards which are reached by steam and sailing vessels of considerable size.

That this place was selected for a town is difficult to understand. It probably was the result of an accidental circumstance. Fort Dearborn was built at the mouth of the Chicago River to control the Indians and was probably the nucleus of a trading post many years ago, and around this centred what has become one of the most important cities in the United States. Chicago means in Indian "skunk," probably because the locality was a low, marshy, miasmatic, "stinking" place, and more applicable to the river now than when the fort was built. The travel in the city as well as sanitary considerations I have no doubt will ultimately require it to be filled up, and the shipping interests transferred to the lake front.

I had almost forgotten to mention the Corn and Wheat Exchange which to one who has not been present during hours in a Stock Exchange will be very interesting. From this place as a great grain centre the pulse of the market is sometimes felt all over the world. In a large room in the Exchange are two circles about 15 feet in diameter each surrounded by a narrow elevated platform reached by a few steps on the outside of the circle and a similar number on the inside, thus forming what are known as the "corn and wheat pits." Into these the brokers gather in large numbers, and if there is any excitement either from panic or boom, then to the uninitiated there arises a jargon of sounds, so vociferous and unintelligible, accompanied with evidences of the greatest excitement, that the most turbulent mob or the wildest demonstration in an insane asylum would be mildness itself in comparison. After hours there are often gatherings in the streets in the immediate vicinity and the same demonstrations and transactions are made and this too regardless of the state of the weather. These gatherings are probably made up of irregular dealers and brokers not connected with the exchange.

Having seen as much of the most important objects as we could considering the heat, we prepared to return and started for the Union Depot of which all Chicagoans are very proud and flatter themselves into the belief that it is the finest in the country. We took a train on the Pittsburg, Ft. Wayne and Chicago Railroad to Pittsburg, and from there by Pennsylvania Central to Bainbridge, where we settled down to rest.

On September 1st, I entered my place of business in Philadelphia and like Phileas Fogg after his journey around the world in eighty days was prepared to say, "Here I am, gentlemen," and ready again for business; having travelled by rail and stage nearly 10,000 miles and without the slightest accident, though we had been in places of considerable danger. We had been on narrow guage railways, on correspondingly narrow ledges of rock high up on the almost perpendicular mountain side, where a broken rail or other accident meant almost certain death (and most of the railroads among the mountains of Colorado are narrow gauge), and I will repeat a story I read in an eastern paper since our return which is said to have transpired on one of the roads we went over and serves as an excellent illustration.

"Leaving Salida, we have to use two large mogul engines"—they must have been little moguls for this is a narrow gauge road—"to take us over Marshall Pass, a grade 26 miles long, and 217 feet to the mile"—the grade on the Alleghenies

from Altoona to Cresson does not exceed 96 feet to the mile if we remember aright—"winding around twenty-six degree curves. One side you look down 3,000 feet, while by looking up on the other side of the train you can see rocks hanging over you more than a mile high, one of the grandest sights man ever saw, and worth the time and expense of any man. Forty-four miles is counted a day's work on this division for engineers, and their monthly earnings amount to from $160 to $225, and the risks they run and ability required are worth all the money they get.

"It is here our old friend 'Curley' Whitney had his runaway. Curley was coming down this grade when his brakes got out of order and his train got the start of him. He was running a second section, and seeing no hopes of avoiding collision by dashing into the train ahead, he and his fireman, after doing all they could to check the speed of their train, jumped off and let it go. Ahead of them on the first section was one of those ever wide awake, careful men who always looks to both ends of his train, and he was looking back when Curley and his fireman jumped off. Realizing his danger at once he eased up on his brakes and got the speed of the runaway train. He then caught them and held both trains until he brought them to a full stop."

An accident similar to this is liable at any time, and it can be readily imagined how dangerous it would be even though there might be no chance of collision with another train. We have been in deep canons with overhanging rocks, and from the loose ones at the bottom we knew they must have come from above. We have been on wagon roads only wide enough for the vehicle, on the edges of steep declivities; proximity to elevations from which huge boulders sometimes fall, (one weighing many tons fell a short distance back of the hotel in the Yosemite Valley while we were there, with a noise like thunder and a trembling of the ground.) We got through safely and are thankful.

This narration is made without any pretension to its being a literary effort, and is but a plain account of facts of where we went, and how, what we saw, and our impressions. Doubtless there are some errors in our statements and where they occur it is not the result of intention either to lessen, magnify or deceive us in the slightest degree. We may have in some cases been incorrectly informed, for we did not ourselves measure the height of mountains and water-falls, the depth of canons, count people, etc. Many statements will doubtless appear incredible, but we have stated nothing which we believe would not be confirmed by anyone going over the same ground, unless he should say we had not told half the truth. We feel that an adequate description is impossible to fully impress a reader or hearer with the greatness, the beauty, the sublimity, the wildness, the desolation which we have seen and passed through.

We were impressed with the greatness and vastness of this country and felt proud that we could call it ours, though as yet we have seen little of it. Why cross the ocean before viewing those things in our own country which have scarcely a parallel abroad? Those who have means and time should not fail to make this trip, which will be for them a perpetual feast of pleasant recollections, provided it is concluded without accident or other serious episode, any of which are possible anywhere; but let us here advise (while we do so without vanity) those who contemplate travel here or elsewhere that it is time well spent to procure all the available means of informa-

tion about the places to be visited, and objects to be seen by books of travel, guide books, etc., to peruse them carefully before starting and if necessary make memoranda, because much is passed over by the stranger in strange places without them. What is common and uninteresting to the resident may have particular attractions to the visitor. Indeed residents often do not see the attractions of their own towns or vicinity until some non-resident relative or friend appears, and they then act as guide.

This account was primarily written for ourselves as a record of our trip, and has given us many hours of pleasure in elaborating the details not contained in our diary, which was rather an extended memorandum from day to day, of our doings, and noted every evening when possible. The courteous editor of the CLARION solicited it for the benefit of his subscribers among whom we number many friends. Our own purpose has been accomplished and if we have contributed anything to their pleasure we are pleased that we gave them the record of our

"SUMMER TRIP ACROSS THE CONTINENT."